Surfing Heaven

Cover art by James Richards of Columbia, TN
Author's note: "Surfing Heaven" was originally written in 1995.

Copyright © 2006 Phillip Cothran
All rights reserved.
ISBN:1-4196-2927-1

To order additional copies, please contact us.
BookSurge, LLC
www.booksurge.com
1-866-308-6235
orders@booksurge.com

Surfing Heaven
"an afterlife adventure…"

Phillip Cothran

2006

Surfing Heaven

Dedicated to the strong women in my life...

Prologue

It was just past midnight at Seaview Nursing Home. Howard Robinson, in his white uniform and black dress shoes, was making his midnight rounds. He had to make sure all the old farts were asleep and not up to any mischief. Last night he'd caught Charlie Stempel crawling into bed with Mrs. McPeak, trying to get a little. These folks still had a spark of life in them-a hard, hot spark-but tonight looked like it was going to be quiet. A few heavy snorers and a wet bed wasn't much for a Friday night.

Howard looked down at his shoes and saw they needed shining, as if he had the time. He was already working three jobs and had six kids to feed. He reached into his pocket and pulled out a cigarette. Someone was walking towards him down the darkened hallway. The man was carrying a large white surfboard under his arm.

"Mr. Barr? Jake? Is that you?" Howard asked. The old guy had scared the dickens out of him again.

Ninety-five year-old Jake Barr, adorned only in his underwear and clutching the cumbersome relic from his past, came to a standstill. There was the hint of a sheepish grin on his wrinkled face. Once a body of muscle, he'd turned into a decaying ghost of his former self.

"Let's get you back into your bed, Jake. Out here in your undies. You're gonna give somebody a stroke."

Jake stood his ground.

"I'm going surfing, Howard, that's all. Why won't you let me go surfing?" Jake's voice was beginning to crack. "You said you'd let me go."

"You ain't goin surfin' this time of the night. Now let's get you back into your room before you wake up all these night folks. You wouldn't want to do that, would you?"

Jake gave in as Howard took the board and led him back to room 40. A single golden trophy sitting on the dresser stood as the only reminder he was once one of the world's greatest surfers. A small lamp on the bedside table casts its glow on a glass containing Jake's teeth. Howard rested the surfboard in a corner and helped Jake into bed. ***This guy is one wrinkled up old prune...too much sun in his time probably.***

Jake reached over and put his teeth into his mouth. He lay back against his pillows, staring at Howard. The slight grin had returned, and a weird glimmer was forming in his eyes.

Howard was tense. He needed that cigarette. He reached down and turned off the lamp, then headed for the door.

"Goodnight, Mr. Barr."

Howard had almost escaped when the lamp came back on.

"This is my year, Howard."

Howard spun around. "Jake, please turn that light off."

"I'm going surfing again this year, Howard." His grin had turned into a beaming smile showcasing the pearly dentures.

Howard walked over next to the bed. "Well, you sure are, sir, you sure are." He needed to get this guy settled down so he could finish his rounds. He also needed that cigarette. "Did you take your medication tonight, Jake?"

"Can I tell you a story, Howard?" Jake was leaning towards him now, only inches away.

"It's awful late for stories, Jake. I think you should save it for someone tomorrow. I'm sure Mr. Brown would love to hear it first thing in the morn' over bacon 'n' eggs."

The smile left Jake's face. "There might not be a tomorrow." Jake raised one of his hands towards Howard's chest, shaking it. "I know for a fact I'm going to die this year. I can tell you why." The old man began to tremble.

Howard sat down in the chair next to the bed. The old geezer needed some calming down.

"Okay, Jake, it's twelve-thirty. I'm outta here by one and this better be good." *What the hell, the old fellow never has any visitors. Wouldn't hurt to give him a few minutes.* "Mind if I smoke, Jake?"

"Hell no, I'm almost dead anyway." The grin had returned.

Howard lit the cigarette. The smell filled the room.

Jake relaxed again into his pillows. His face took on a serious expression. "In the early 90's I was the number one surfer on the planet. I had the fame, the money, and the women. It was a helluva life." He reached down and pulled an old yellowed magazine from under the mattress. He pointed to the cover. "That's me." He handed it to Howard.

―※―

The tanned, muscle-toned man on the cover of the surfing magazine looked nothing like the fossil in front of him. "Jake Barr wins at the Pipe," Robinson read. "Well, I'll be. All of this bull you've been tellin' everybody around here is true then?"

"Every damn word," Jake answered. "It all changed one Saturday morning, though."

"What changed? You got a real job?" Howard snickered.

"I had an afterlife experience, you boob."

"Okay, okay, don't get excited. An afterlife experience and you saw God or something...became a monk, huh?" Howard was enjoying himself. He tried to wipe the smile off his face.

"No, nothing like that. I'll start at the beginning. But first, give me a hit off that cigar, will ya?"

Against better judgment, Howard leaned over and let Jake take a hit.

"Ahh, that's better. The bastards around here won't let me have a Coke, let alone a smoke, damn them."

Howard laughed.

"Okay, the story. It all started near here in Southern California. Back in 1996..."

Chapter 1

Jake Barr was flying down a liquid mountain, a mountain of a wave. Surfing down the steep glass, thirty-foot face, he felt no fear, just a serene calm. Bracing himself, he did a bottom turn and headed for the monster's shoulder. There was no shoulder. The towering face of water continued on indefinitely and was beginning to break over him as he slashed back and forth near the bottom. A loud rumble filled his ears. The wave closed in on him. *Should I bail out? Just dive deep, hold my breath, and hope I come up behind this mountain?* It was now or never.

He stayed on the board. Tons of ocean thundered over him. He found himself still riding the board, inside an endless tube of liquid. The board seemed to be going by itself down the tunnel as though searching for an exit for its rider. Jake walked around on the board. Everything was slowing down, as if in slow motion. He stood looking at the sides of the tube, the water flowing around him in green and blue glowing colors. Was that his reflection distorted in the side? A tanned man with short, blonde hair smiled back at him. Jake looked back toward the front of the surfboard, wondering if he'd emerge back into daylight. Something or someone was coming towards him. Another surfer…

The other surfer was calling his name. A sense of fear swept over Jake. The rider was closing on him. *Who is it? Why am I afraid?* The figure was hazy, dressed in black, as though the grim reaper himself had taken up the sport. The rider kept calling his name. Jake began to lose his balance.

He dropped to one knee as the board began to roll slowly over and out of control. The dark rider was upon him.

"Are you running again, Jake? You can't run forever," the dark rider shouted.

Jake went tumbling into the side of the tube while hideous laughter followed him.

The tortuous cry of the alarm clock sounded. It was the weird dream again. He'd been having this same dream for the past few weeks. He reached over and silenced the clock. It was time to get up and do the dawn patrol boogie. *Hit the surf early, establish my spot in the lineup and surf 'til afternoon.* He struggled into the bathroom. *You look like shit. A few too many beers last night, or what?* After a failed attempt at dragging the comb through his hair, he used his fingers to untangle the blonde mess.

He slipped on his wetsuit and headed for the kitchen. In the hallway he passed rows of polished, golden trophies that saluted his deeds. They had passed the point of meaning anything anymore, and were now just part of the furniture filling the small apartment. In the kitchen, he wolfed down some cold pizza and chased it with an icy beer.

Charlie Sims would be there any minute to pick him up. They'd been surfing together since they were kids. Besides, Jake didn't have a car. Why ever buy one? He was always on the road, surfing the circuit. Between contests he was anywhere on the planet that had waves to catch. The women were also willing. Jake never went too long without a new girlfriend who happily drove him anywhere, usually to a good surf spot where she'd wait for hours until he came out of the water.

Some didn't wait. He would emerge from the water to find them gone and himself looking for a ride back. His last girlfriend had moved out only two days earlier. Couldn't handle the lifestyle, she'd said, and was gone, along with Jake's CD collection. A car horn was sounding outside.

Jake grabbed his board and looked out the window. Charlie was sitting there in his jeep, flashing his contagious smile. Jake locked up the apartment.

"You ready, champ?" Charlie laughed as Jake walked up.

"Hell no, it's too early, you asshole." Jake fastened his board atop Charlie's on the jeep's roof and jumped in. Charlie hit the accelerator and squealed out of the parking lot.

Charlie was a damned good surfer—maybe even better than himself—but he chose not to compete. He preferred to remain a "soul surfer," and shunned competition as if it were unclean. It was his loss, Jake had always told him. Charlie would just smile, shake his head, and say, "You'll understand one day, or not."

On this morning they were driving to a spot up north known to only a few surfers. Eventually word would get out and the place would be overrun. The traffic was light heading up the coast. They passed by fewer than the usual number of BMWs and Jags. The streets and sidewalks were still bare of the weekend circus of skaters, mimes, muscle flexors and the other off mixture of characters these parts attracted.

Charlie was also wearing a wetsuit. The skies were overcast and the water would be chilly. Charlie's red hair was cut in a Marine-like, buzz cut. He'd earned the nickname "Carrot" as a kid, but Jake only called him that when he was drunk.

A report came over the radio warning of high surf and choppy conditions. The excited voice went on to say that wave heights would be in the ten to twelve-foot range.

There was a hurricane named Emily several hundred miles out in the Pacific and she was not in a good mood.

"Sounds good to me," Jake said. "Less kooks in the water."

"Come on man, you were a kook once yourself. They gotta start somewhere."

"Not on a day like this."

Charlie looked at the surf crashing into a seawall at their left. "Yeah, somebody could die out there today," Charlie said.

Charlie exited off the freeway and was soon driving down a street lined with glass and wooden beach homes. He parked the jeep in front of one of the houses. The spot was behind private property and not yet accessible to the public. A friend of Charlie's lived here and had given him permission to pass through the yard anytime he felt like it, as long as the place remained a secret. They got their boards, quietly opened the gate in the fence and passed through the neatly manicured back yard. Another gate in the rear led them to a grassy knoll where they stood facing the ocean.

The awakening sea spread out before them. A strong wind blew from the west. The sun was barely up behind them. A set of waves bore down on a point extending from a small hill two hundred yards up the beach. They quietly started down a dirt trail which soon turned into sand. It felt cool to their feet, not yet warmed by the June sun. Their footprints left a path across the beach that led to the water's edge. The sea looked turbulent. The shorebreak was pounding into the beach. It would be tough, paddling out to where the waves were breaking. They could see two figures bobbing in the water out past the point.

"Only two guys out there," Charlie said.

"That makes four of us crazy enough to be out here this early," Jake replied.

They attached their ankle leashes and stood waiting for a lull in the shorebreak. Finally the water smoothed out.

"Let's do it!" Charlie shouted. They both yelled like wild men and ran into the sea. The water was cold. The wetsuit helped but the exposed feet and head would feel it. They pushed down on their boards and dived under a wave, coming up behind as it rolled by and crashed into shore. They paddled up and over choppy hills. After a few minutes of battling through the drunken sea they were at the point. A man rode past them on a wave of about twelve feet in height. The man ignored them as they paddled by. Jake watched as the guy disappeared behind the wave.

Jake and Charlie sat astride their boards, feet dangling in the dark waters, oblivious to what could be lurking below them. Shark attacks were few and far between. *Besides, they always get the other guy.*

The rhythm of the sea pushed them slowly up and down as if they were in a huge cradle of water. *It's the beginning of a day like hundreds of others.* Jake watched the horizon for an incoming set. A hill formed, slowly moving and growing as it approached them. The two men began to paddle furiously, battling for position. It was upon them. Jake pushed off at the top and went down the crest of the wave as it broke to his left. He turned right, slashing his board up and down the shoulder, then turning back into its mouth and out again. He rode the wave a few more seconds, then bailed out behind as it began to die. As he paddled toward the point, he could see Charlie catching a nice wave on the horizon.

By noon they were both getting a little tired. The

choppy water made them work harder. They sat on their boards watching the horizon.

"So, what are you doing this summer?" Charlie asked. "No more contests 'til the fall."

"Maybe I'll catch a flight to Fiji. Or just stay here and stay drunk. I don't know."

"Heard from your mom lately?"

"She's still living in Iowa." Jake answered. "Good ol' land-locked Iowa.

"How long since you seen her?"

"Shit, I don't know-couple of years. Why?" Jake was getting agitated.

"Just asking. Do you ever call?" Charlie continued, knowing he could get away with it.

Jake looked towards the horizon as a set slowly began to form. "Yeah, I call."

His mother, brother and sister had moved back to Iowa years earlier, after the "incident." There was no way he was going back to land-locked Iowa. It was the middle of nowhere with no ocean in sight. So at the age of fourteen he'd moved in with his Aunt and stayed in L.A., while the rest of his family returned home. It took a lot of persuading, but his mother had finally given in. Shit, he'd already won a few amateur surf meets by that time and he knew where his future lay. It wasn't in Iowa.

"Let's catch the next set in and go home. I've had enough, Charlie."

"Okay, man. But hey, call your mom."

Jake was paddling away. "What?" he yelled back.

A large menacing set was closing on them.

"Call your mom, you asshole."

Looking back at Charlie, Jake held a hand to his ear and shook his head.

The set looked larger than any he'd seen all morning. The second hill looked even bigger. He went over the first. Looking back, he glimpsed Charlie taking off and disappearing in front of the first wave. The other guy was paddling his ass off and closing. They were both picked up. Jake pushed off and rose to his feet, beginning a steep descent. The other guy had given up.

Jake coasted down the face of the wave. Doing a bottom turn, he looked up and watched as the giant began to break over him. He was in the tube! He put out his hand and felt the side as he ducked the wall above him. He felt a sudden jerk at his ankle leash. *What the hell?* He looked down. There was nothing there. The leash looked fine. He was almost out of the tube when the leash jerked again. This one caused him to lose his balance and he fell into the water. The wave poured into him. He was launched into oblivion.

Jake held his breath. He could hear his heart—the only sound in the darkness—pounding away. Suddenly his head jerked forward and a deep pain shot through his skull. The board had struck him. He took in some water. Even as he tried to regain his senses, his body tumbled out of control, pulling the traitorous surfboard along behind. He was a bug in God's washing machine.

His body had quit tumbling. He was now gently revolving through dark liquid space. It felt warm and assuring, like being back in the womb, but with a surfboard connected to his ankle. He felt a tightness in his chest as he tried to breathe. He opened his mouth. No water rushed in. *I'm still under water, aren't I?* A faint light shimmered above. *The surface!* He tried but couldn't coax his body to swim upwards. *Oh God, I must be paralyzed!* The thought raged inside him. The light started to fade as he kept revolving in the dark. Dizzy and disoriented, Jake passed into the void.

Chapter 2

Jake was floating in a calm, warm sea. He felt drowsy but some small sensations were creeping back into his body. To his relief, he could wiggle his toes. He was on his back, the water splashing around him. He felt two arms extending underneath his limp body.

Someone was gently carrying him through the water. He opened his mouth but no words would come out. He cracked open an eye. It was barely light out. A blurry figure looked down at him. It appeared to be a woman. He was being carried by a woman! Charlie was probably rolling on the beach, laughing his ass off. Jake Barr being carried out of the surf by a female—he would never live it down. He closed his eye and drifted off again into neverland.

Chapter 3

Jake was peddling his bike as fast as it would go. His legs went up and down like two pistons. At thirteen years old, he could only stay out until six o'clock on a school night. It was 6:15 and he hadn't been home since early that Sunday morning. Lately he stayed away from the house as much as possible. His parents were fighting. He hated to hear them yell and threaten each other.

The red brick house came into view. *Just keep peddling. Find another house to live in—one with a happy family, like ours used to be.* He pulled the bike into his yard. With no cars in the driveway, the house looked deserted. He walked up to the front door. It was locked. *Where is everyone?* There was always the rear window. He knew how to pry that open.

Jake walked past a row of his mother's yellow tulips to the side gate. He could hear the low idle of a car engine nearby. There was no car to be seen. The noise seemed to be drifting from behind the gate. He opened the wooden gate and entered the back yard. He was startled to see his father's green station wagon sitting in the middle of the yard.

The engine was running but the car was just sitting there. *Why would Dad just leave his car running like that?* He walked towards the car. He noticed a red rag hanging out of the exhaust pipe. The windows of the car were blurry. Walking up to the front of the car he could see a figure hunched over in the driver's seat and pressed up against the window. A grip of horror seized his young mind. He turned and ran out through the gate. He jumped on the yellow bike and peddled away, never looking back.

Jake's eyes fluttered open. He had tried to block it out for so long, and now he'd dreamed it again. There was whiteness everywhere. He was lying in a bed of clean, white sheets surrounded by four, white walls. One had an open window. To his left, there was an archway that opened into a hall. He sat up on his elbows. He was in a strange bed, feeling a little hung over. It wasn't the first time.

He was still wearing the black wetsuit and was barefooted. The suit was dry. He swung his legs over the bed's edge and stood up uneasily in the middle of the small room. There was a pile of clothes, neatly folded at the foot of the bed. A pair of sandals rested next to the clothing. He walked over and picked up a shirt from the pile. The clothes were his. Two surfboards were leaning up in a corner of the room. He walked up to them. These, too, were his belongings. *This must be some kind of joke.*

Jake walked over to the window, attempting to get his bearings. The ocean stretched out below him. The window looked down a grassy hill and then became a wide, white, sandy beach. The water looked a lot calmer than it had been earlier. The sun was perched above the horizon of the ocean, but if it was setting, why did it feel like morning to him? He could see waves breaking up the coast. It was odd that no one was out there surfing, as the waves looked smooth and glassy. In fact, the entire length of the beach was deserted.

"I don't know this beach," he said softly to himself. There appeared to be a patch of land on the horizon. *Is it a small island?* A sailboat was half the distance to the island. Jake turned and walked towards the doorway, looking for a clue as to where he was. *Maybe this place has a phone.*

"Hello! Is anyone here?" he called out.

In the middle of the next room was a small round table

flanked by a couple of cushioned reading chairs. A large bookcase holding hundreds of volumes of all colors and sizes, filled one wall. On a whim, Jake reached up, pulled one out, and looked at its cover. *"The Wizard of Oz,* by Frank Baum," he said softly. He had watched it on TV as a kid, but had never read the book. He opened it and thumbed through the pages, pausing to look at illustrations of the scarecrow, some flying monkeys, and the Emerald City. He closed the book and placed it back into its slot on the shelf.

Jake looked around and saw another room like the first, with bland white walls and no pictures or personality. On the opposite wall, a large archway covered by curtains led out to a balcony. There was a closed door which probably led out to the front. He walked to the archway, pulled the white silky curtains apart and went out onto the balcony. A warm light breeze hit him. The air smelled strange. It smelled clean. Looking up the beach, he saw the tiny outline of another house. He went back inside and walked over by the small table. I have to get out of here. *Whoever lives here might come back and I don't want to be here when they do.* The place gave him the creeps.

He looked at the table. A couple of blue, palm-sized rocks were lying on it. He picked up one of them. It felt smooth and warm. He could see through it, holding it up to the light coming in from the archway. He laid the stone back on the table. It was time to get out of there. Remembering the boards and clothing, he ran back into the bedroom. He scooped up the clothes under one arm while clumsily positioning the boards under the other. He ran out with his load, somehow managing to close the door behind him. He didn't notice that the blue stone he'd held moments before was now glowing brightly on the table.

Chapter 4

Stretching before him was a path of fine, red gravel which led into the trees and disappeared. Jake turned and looked back at the house. It was a white, stucco cottage with a blue tile roof. *Not your typical, rich Southern California beach home.* On the door he noticed a brass plaque like those marking fine English homes. It read:

J. Barr
1970-2065

He rubbed his hand across the raised letters and numbers. It felt ancient. This joke was getting sicker. Charlie was probably standing behind a tree watching him.

"Charlie!" he shouted. "Where are you?"

It was quiet—too quiet. There wasn't a bird singing or an insect chirping—just the distant sound of ocean washing its waves on the beach below the house. He now remembered the wipeout and the feeling of being carried out of the water. He looked back at the plaque. *Why has someone put my name on there?* The *Wizard of Oz* popped back into his thoughts. *Wonder if there's a pair of spindly legs sticking out from under the house?*

He had to find a phone. He started up the path towards the trees. The gravel felt smooth and warm to his feet, comfortable as a bed. The grass along the path gave way to thick, dark bushes and a forest beyond. He entered the forest.

The trees were an odd mixture of tall pines, towering, thick oaks, and waving palms. There was another tree he couldn't identify. Hanging from its branches were hundreds of yellow, palm-sized fruit. Still, all was quiet. He'd expected to hear at least a bird here in the woods. He kept walking, constantly adjusting the two surfboards under his left arm. The path led to another which forked right and left. Remembering the other house up the beach, he turned left.

This new path, wider than the first, was nearly six feet across. The boards were beginning to weigh down upon him. He decided to hide them in the trees. Walking into the forest undergrowth, leaves and small twigs crunching under his feet, he looked for a spot. He found a place near the exposed roots of a huge oak. Jake placed the boards on the ground and covered them with oak leaves and a couple of large, fallen palm branches.

He went back to the path and journeyed deeper into the forest. *That house up the beach can't be too far away.* Rounding a curve he came face to face with a short, pudgy Chinaman. The man was wearing no shirt, just red, Bermuda shorts and a pair of sandals.

"Excuse me. Is there a pay phone around here?" Jake asked as the two came together.

The man's solemn expression turned into an angry stare. He started shouting and waving his arms about. Jake stepped back a couple of paces. The Chinaman pointed a finger at Jake and let loose another torrent of curses. The man quickened his step and passed Jake, looking back over his shoulder and shouting. The fellow disappeared from view around a bend.

"Thank you, Good Samaritan," Jake called after him. He turned and continued on. *What's eating that guy?*

At the next fork, a narrower path like the first one he'd been on peeled off to the right. The wide path kept running parallel to the sea. He decided to stay on course for the other beach home.

After several minutes of walking, he came to a trail that led in the direction of the water. Through the thinning trees he could see the other house at the ocean's edge. He quickened his steps. To his left, standing among bushes, was a lady with her back to him. She was staring in the direction of the house. He left the path and walked towards the woman, stopping a few feet behind her.

"Percy! Perrrccceey!"

"Excuse me. Sorry to interrupt you, but do you live here?"

The woman turned quickly, as if she'd been caught in some unseemly deed. She had long, golden hair and a pretty face. Her loose, long white gown was almost like a toga. She stood for a few seconds, staring at Jake, then suddenly laughed and darted away through the bushes. Jake was beginning to wonder if he'd stumbled into an asylum. He got back on the path and headed for the house.

This house was similar to the first one. Another plain, white stucco with a blue tile roof. At the front door he found another plaque. It read:

P. Shelley

1792-1822

Maybe it's just some kind of weird address system they use around here. There was always something new in California. He brought his hand up and knocked on the door.

Chapter 5

The door opened and a man stood there. He was slight of figure with large blue eyes, and curly deep brown hair. He stood barefooted, wearing a pair of faded blue jeans and a loose unbuttoned white shirt. Jake opened his mouth to speak.

"Hello. I..."

"Have you ever read "Queen Mab?" the man interrupted Jake.

"Uhh...no,"

"How about, 'The Revolt of Islam?' You must have read that poem."

"Who's revolting?" Jake was confused. He took a step backwards.

"Oh, never mind." The man looked down at his feet.

"Poetry is dead, and so am I," the man mumbled.

"Look, I'll just leave and..."

The stranger's eyes widened. "*Frankenstein*. Ever heard of *Frankenstein*?" the man continued.

"Everyone's heard of *Frankenstein*."

"Mary became immortal, and I nothing." The fellow looked down again as if he were about to cry.

Jake was getting worried. *What's this guy up to? I should just turn around and leave.* The man looked up again, smiling.

"Percy Bysshe Shelley, at your service."

"Jake Barr. Can I use your telephone?"

A look of shock broke over Shelley's face. "Jake Barr? Jake Barr! Come in quickly, you're in great danger." Shelley grabbed Jake by the arm and pulled him into the house.

They were standing in a large, white room. Shelves full of books lined one wall. Two cushioned chairs with a small, round table between them sat in the middle of the room. Curtains were drawn back to expose an archway leading to a balcony. Jake was stunned. It was just like the other house. Shelley peeped out a small window by the front door.

"Did you see anyone odd outside?" Shelley asked, turning back to Jake.

"A couple of people. You're making me a little nervous, too."

"What did they look like?" Shelley demanded. He left the window and stood a few inches away from Jake.

"There was a Chinese guy who seemed pretty pissed off about something."

"That was Lee Wu. He died in the Boxer Rebellion. He was killed by an American soldier. You're an American."

"Uhh, yeah," Jake answered. Something wasn't right here.

"Wu has never gotten over the circumstances surrounding his death. I'd keep my distance from him if I were you."

Jake edged closer to the door. *This guy is definitely a looney.* There was something scribbled all over the walls, not unlike the bathroom walls back in his high school. He couldn't make out the faded words.

"Who else? What about a woman?" Shelley stayed with him and tried to get in between Jake and the front door.

"Yeah, a woman. She was standing in the bushes watching your house." Jake reached for the doorknob.

"Harriet!" Shelley's eyes widened. He ran back to the window, his head moving back and forth as if watching a high speed tennis match. "That damned woman will haunt me forever." He looked back at Jake who had cracked the door open. "I was not responsible for her suicide."

"You're insane." Jake threw open the door and ran outside. He looked back to see if the man was following him.

Shelley ran out and stopped just outside the door. "Come back! They'll get you! You're in danger, my friend!"

Jake turned and faced him, cocking his arm back just in case.

"I'm not your friend. Your mother should be shot for naming you Percy." He put his arm down, turned, and started back up the trail.

"Beware the men in black!" he called after Jake. "The men in black! I'm trying to warn you!"

Jake turned around and glanced back. The kook had quit following him. He'd come close to eating a Jake Barr fist. *Maybe if I keep running in one direction I'll come to the electric fence and the guards will let me out.* He figured he was in some loony bin or fruitcake religious commune. *The men in black, my ass.* He walked on.

Jake soon came to a wide, red-brick road that broke off from the main path along the sea. The bricks were neatly in place and retained their color as if they'd been recently laid. Although the way looked inviting, the bricks were harder on Jake's feet. He was tempted to go back and grab the sandals that he'd hidden.

The sun climbed above him, signaling noon. He was wiping a line of sweat off his forehead when it began to sink in; the sun had been just above the horizon when he'd awakened earlier, yet now it was above him. *If this is California, the sun should have gone down.* He stopped and looked around. *My name on the door of a strange house. Weird people ranting nonsense. Where the hell am I?* The forest hovered over the road where he stood, coming together overhead and blocking most of the light.

As he walked, Jake looked around nervously. There were still no bird or insect sounds coming from the trees. In the eerie silence, he kept imagining that a head was peeking out from behind a tree trunk, or that someone was watching from the branches above. He quickened his steps. Buildings came into view ahead.

He walked up the red-brick road between two small, wooden buildings. Two similar structures stood to his north, another to the west. He walked out into the middle of the place. Four brick roads came together in the center of the village, forming a crossroads.

There wasn't a sound or a person anywhere. He looked closely at the buildings. They were very plain, like something out of the Old West. On each building was a small wooden sign identifying it. The one to the southeast said "Café." He walked a few paces toward it and found that the front opened onto a courtyard of rustic tables and chairs. A few more tables were under an extending roof. The front was open and exposed. There didn't appear to be any bar or counter. No employees were around to serve would-be patrons. Small bowls, filled with the fruit he'd seen hanging in the forest, had been placed on each table. He wasn't hungry, but on a whim he picked up a piece. It was yellow and fit smoothly in the palm of his hand. There was a soft feel to it, as if it were spoiled. He brought the fruit to his mouth and took a bite. It was delicious. He took another bite.

He walked back towards the crossroads. The sign on the building to the northeast read, "Books." *I'll pass on that one.* The building to the southwest said, "Clothes." The two buildings to the northwest read, "Pools," and "Inn." *Where there's an inn, there must be an innkeeper.* He walked towards the inn, taking another bite of the fruit on the way. The door of the inn had a sign reading, "Welcome, Travelers." He pressed hesitantly, and slowly the door opened. Jake looked in. There were no lights on, but he could make out a long counter. He entered, leaving the door open so he'd have some light. The counter was wooden, and had four guest registers and a pen resting on top. There was no one in sight.

"Hello, is anyone here?" There was no answer. He looked down at the registers. One said, "Visitors." The next read, "Past Residents," and was thicker. The third said, "Present Residents." He opened it and read:

Name/Nationality/Occupation/Earth Years
Pierre Boulanger/French/Artist/1871-1937
Eleonora Farinelli/Italian/Wife/1910-1991
Koji Fukudu/Japanese   /Soldier/1920-1944
Mekita Kenot/Ethiopian/Farmer/1902-1936
Olga Yuenich/Russian/Nurse/1890-1966
Percy Shelley/English   /Poet/1792-1822
Newt Worley/American/Soldier/1948-1968
Maria Quintero/Mexican/Wife/1861-1935
Singing Wind/Sioux/Hunter/1788-1850
Lee Wu/Chinese/Farmer/1874-1900
Hector Munoz   /Cuban/Fisherman/1899-1972
Balsam Bayar/Turkish/Wife/1923-1994
Emily Adams/American/Daughter/1853-1870
Kali Ahmad/Egyptian   /Prostitute/1922-1961
Ai-ling Quan/Chinese/Wife/1768-1869
Kari Swenson/Norwegian/Teacher/1890-1979
Nguyen Van Phu/Vietnamese   /Farmer/1898-1970

It was just a single page of names he'd never heard of. He closed the book. The last register read, "Future Residents."

Its cover felt like an old discarded photo album. Again there were names listed in one column, followed by nationality, occupation, and "Earth Years." Most of the names he couldn't pronounce. Scanning down the first page he gasped as he read:

Mohammed Aghi/Jordanian/Policeman/1982-2070
Jake Barr/American/Surfer/1970-2065
Max Burns/Australian   /Farmer/1960-2054

He slammed the book shut.

"What the hell's going on here?" He looked to his left and saw the beginning of a hallway. He left the counter and walked to the entrance. Six doors were spaced apart along the hall. He walked over and opened the first. Inside, he could see a small bed and a cushioned chair with a table next to it. There was just enough light to see one of the blue stones sitting on the table. *Maybe I can use it as a weapon.* He went over and picked it up. Stepping back out into the sunlight, Jake headed for the "Pools" building, opened the door, and entered.

The white marble floor was cool to his weary feet. Light shining in through two windows revealed birdbath-like fountains, spaced a few feet apart, across the room. Someone was sitting in a darkened corner.

"Hello. Is there a phone here?" He walked a few feet towards the figure in the corner. The person in the shadows stood and came out into the light.

Jake stared in amazement at the figure of a very old man. Not just old, but someone who looked like he'd lived ten lives. The man was dressed in a white toga which touched his wrinkled feet. A gray beard flowed all the way to his knees, and his long gray hair hung straight to his shoulders. The man's eyes followed Jake hypnotically.

"Do you want to see your death? That's popular," came the words from the sagging mouth.

Suddenly the blue rock in Jake's hand began to glow, filling the room with light and highlighting the ghastly appearance of the old man's wrinkled face. Surprised, Jake dropped the stone. He watched it fall and crack into two pieces on the marble floor.

They flickered and went dark. He quickly looked back up. The old man was walking towards him.

"Do you care to see your death or deal with a sin?" the fossil growled.

Jake braced himself and hurled his half-eaten fruit at the old man, just grazing the guy's shoulder. He turned and ran for the exit.

"I know who you are. We have something special in mind for you."

Jake stopped at the door and looked back. "What the hell are you talking about?"

"There's a purpose for your early arrival. You died for a reason," the old fellow continued.

"I think you're all crazy here!" Jake slammed the door behind him as he ran out towards the crossroads. The old man made no attempt to follow him. After deciding to return to the place he'd awakened earlier, Jake walked to the forest along the red-brick road.

Once again the oak and palm trees towered over him. Dark shadows shifted between the trunks, but he saw no one. He was nearly convinced that his mind was playing tricks on him when two figures emerged from the trees ahead.

They were dressed in black cloaks. Jake's immediate impulse was to run, but he wasn't the type to run from a fight. Besides, the two could be friendly for all he knew. They were walking towards him.

"Jake Barr?" one asked. Their faces were smiling. They were very pale and could have passed for twins. The cloaks covered their bodies down to their feet, upon which they wore white tennis shoes.

"Yes," Jake responded.

"We're here to help you. We know you're lost and need assistance," the other one said.

"Where am I? Where's Charlie, and how did I get here?"

Both of them laughed. "Of course you have a lot of questions," the first one said, "but right now you need medical treatment and a good meal. Come with us."

The men flanked Jake, turned him around, and headed back towards the village. As the three made their way slowly up the road, Jake remembered the crazy old coot in the village and decided he didn't want to go back there. He looked nervously back and forth at the two men. *The temperature must be near a hundred, so why are these guys in heavy robes? Shelley warned me to beware of the men in black.*

"Wait. I left some things back down the trail. I need to go get them," Jake said.

"No time for a surfboard. He is waiting." They each put a hand on Jake's shoulders.

Jake quickly shifted backwards, pulling the two men off balance and causing them to lose their grip on him. He swung a fist at one of them, catching the guy on the chin and sending him spiraling to the ground.

"How'd you guys know about the surfboard?" he asked. The hood of the fallen man was down around his neck. He was bald and his scalp had a red cross painted on it. Jake had seen gang members with strange tattoos, but nothing like this. The stunned man rolled over on his side, moaning, and trying to lift his body.

The other man pulled an object out of his cloak and came towards Jake. "You shouldn't have done that, Barr!" The man came closer.

"Who are you guys?"

"Why, we're the Red Cross," the man walking towards him snickered.

Jake looked down at the man's hand. It held a red-handled knife with a black blade that curved crazily before reaching a sharp point. He backed up a couple of paces and wiped the sweat from his eyes.

"We had orders to take you alive, but in just such a case as this, we can kill you. Do you feel like dying twice in the same day, Barr?"

Jake glanced back. The other guy was rising to his feet. He was still wobbly. Jake quickly turned as the man with the knife lunged at him. Grabbing hold of his attacker's arm, Jake forced him into his counterpart. The dagger struck the wobbling man in the chest. Jake let go and backed up a few steps. The twins stared for a moment into one another's eyes. The man with the dagger pulled it out of his partner and backed away. A look of horror spread over the impaled, bald man as he grasped at his wound. He fell to the ground and sat there on his knees.

"You've doomed me, Jake Barr. Doomed me to Hell." He fell over on his side. His body quickly turned to a smoking pile of ashes. A light breeze blew his remains along the ground and into the air.

The black robe lay among the ashes. The other man had pocketed the dagger and was running into the woods.

Jake walked up to the pile of ashes and lifted the robe. "I'm definitely not in California," he said softly.

He decided to go back and talk to Shelley.

Chapter 6

Jake turned off the path that hugged the coast, and approached Shelley's house. He walked up to the front door. Before knocking he paused to look around and make sure he'd not been followed. Nothing stirred near the house or among the trees. He knocked on the door. No one answered. Again, he knocked. Still, no Percy. He tried the bronze door handle. It was unlocked. He slowly pushed the door open and walked into the front room, pulling it shut behind him. There was no sign of anyone.

"Hello. Percy, are you here?"

A book lay on the seat of one of the chairs. Jake bent over and picked it up. *The Divine Comedy,* by Dante Alighieri. He opened the book and thumbed through the pages. He stopped at one picture of several people being led around in chains by some demonic looking creatures. *Dante was that guy who went to Hell and lived to tell about it, or something like that.*

"He wasn't even close."

Jake dropped the book and looked up in surprise. Percy stood in the archway, the curtains blowing around him. He walked toward Jake.

"Think about it. His medieval mind produced a medieval vision," Shelley continued.

"What?" Jake was getting worried. He'd hoped this guy would make some sense.

"Oh, come on, man. Haven't you figured it out yet?"

Jake was confused and angry at the same time. "I know there's something weird going on around this place and I want some answers. Your men in black jumped me a few minutes ago. I took out one of them and the guy's body just dissolved. His body just vanished into a pile of dust."

Percy was shocked. "A pile of dust? And the other one?"

"He ran away, into the woods."

"They know you're here on this island now. They'll be back." Agitated, he began to walk back and forth across the room, pausing to look out the front window.

"Who are they? What do you mean, 'island'? I was surfing nowhere near an island this morning. Why would those guys want to hur...?"

"One question at a time, my friend." Percy left the window and smiled as he walked past Jake. "Come out on the balcony and sit with me. We need to talk."

They walked through the white flowing curtains and onto a wide, stone balcony. Jake went to the railing and stared out at the endless blue waters. A breeze was blowing across the balcony, carrying the smell of the sea with it. The wide, white, sandy beach stretched away in both directions. There wasn't a soul sunbathing, and no children were building sand castles. There were a few good waves rolling in, but not a surfer to be seen. He could still see the other island across the sea, but the sailboat from earlier was gone.

"Is the beach here polluted or something?"

Shelley sat down and beckoned Jake to take the seat next to him. The simple wood frames with their small cushions were not inviting. Jake took another look down the beach. He could see the place he'd awakened in that morning and another house in the opposite direction.

"Who lives there?" he asked, pointing.

"It's empty. The resident is supposed to arrive some time in 2017. It was occupied last by a pleasant, French lady."

Jake walked over and sat down next to Shelley. "Okay, where am I?"

"It's more like where you're not anymore," Shelley replied.

"Can't you give me a straight answer?"

"Sure. You're somewhere between Heaven and Hell."

Jake took a deep breath. He stared at Percy who was smiling back at him. The sun peeped over the roof behind them as sounds of the waves crashed below.

"I'm dead. You're saying I'm dead."

"In the Earth sense, yes. Here, you're alive again. So quit panicking, my good man."

"Where exactly is here? If it isn't Heaven or Hell, what is it?" A bead of sweat ran down Jake's forehead. His heart was racing.

"I wish you hadn't started with that question. All I know is that we're not in either place. No harps or angel wings or fiery pits. We sinned just enough to keep ourselves out of Heaven. Did just enough good to avoid Hell. Some call this place 'Purgatory', others prefer 'Limbo'. I suppose it really doesn't matter."

Jake stood and walked back to the stone railing. "This is too weird. It's not what I learned in Sunday school. It's bullshit."

"Bullshit or not, you're here, my friend, but you're here early. That's the puzzle."

Jake turned, walked back and sat down, wiping the sweat across his forehead. "What do you mean?"

"Did you look at your front door? You're not supposed to be here until 2065. Your presence here in the Earth year 1996 is odd."

"So, I'm supposed to die in the year 2065?"

"Exactly," responded Shelley. "How I love new neighbors. The conversation does get old around here."

"Ninety-five years old. Never thought I'd live that long. Never thought I'd see thirty," Jake muttered.

"But you did...or you will. At least, you should. No one arrives here as you have, before his time. I really can't answer this."

Jake stared down at the waves rolling in below. "So I wiped out on a wave and bought it."

"I'm sorry. I don't understand. Were you in a boating accident?"

"No. I died surfing."

"What's that?"

"What's what?"

"Surfing," Shelley said, confused.

"You don't know what surfing is? When did you get here?"

"1822."

"I have a couple of boards close to here. I'll show you later." Jake looked thoughtful for a moment. "Will we be here forever?"

"Yes and no. From what I've seen, we're here for two hundred years and then, poof! We vanish. I went to Marie's good-bye and watched her leave."

"Marie?"

"The Frenchwoman who used to live next door. She'd been here since the earth year 1770. In 1970, two hundred years to the day of her arrival, a few of us gathered at her house to witness her departure."

"Where did she go?"

"I'm getting to that," Shelley said. "Anyway, she lay in her bed, feeling rather weak, she said, telling us all good-bye and what good company we'd been. Suddenly the very bed she was in started shaking. Well, Marie started to scream but we were helpless with fear to do anything." Shelley was rather dramatic with the hand gestures. "When the bed came to a stop, only her red dress was left. She was gone."

"Where did she go?"

"To Heaven or Hell, I don't know. They say it's determined by how we behave ourselves here."

"They?" Jake asked.

"The apostles. You've met two of them already. The men in black. They move about the islands speaking of redemption."

"They tried to kill me!" Jake cried.

Shelley looked puzzled, a frown crossing his face. "Tried to kill you, did they? They came through here looking for you a few days ago. Seemed to know you were coming but didn't know the exact date. They were strange, not as friendly as usual. Wouldn't even look me in the eye when they asked if I'd seen you, which I hadn't, and they got angry when I told them you weren't supposed to be here for another seventy years."

"Great. I've died and gone to the afterlife and someone has put out a hit on me," Jake said.

"A hit?"

"Someone wants to kill me."

"Well, you are here early. Maybe it's just their way of sending you back," Percy mused, "but there must be a better way." He let out a laugh.

"I don't find it funny," Jake fumed. "So it's just us and these apostle characters?" Jake sank down in the chair, relaxing a bit.

"And the leader of the apostles," Shelley replied.

"Leader?"

"Well, someone has to run things. Don't you think?"

"Okay. Who is this leader?"

Shelley had one foot up on the chair, and was occupied with his toenail. "Around here, we call him 'The Lord of Limbo'."

"Great. This Oz even has a wizard," Jake laughed.

Shelley stopped fiddling with his toe. "It's odd, but no one's seen him. At least, no one I've ever talked to here. The apostles are very tight-lipped. They only say, like Satan, he's another fallen Angel. Whereas Satan was banished from Heaven for being evil, the Lord of Limbo was kicked out because he was so insane. The perfect Angel to run Limbo."

Jake paced back and forth. His head throbbed and he couldn't think. None of this made any sense. He looked out at the island on the horizon. "Who lives over there?" he asked, pointing at it.

"Around twenty other lost souls. There's a small village surrounded by a forest on every island. Thousands of islands, all the same, make up this world. And there's the Isle of Labor."

"Isle of Labor?"

"It's for those who committed suicide on Earth."

Jake's mouth dropped open.

"You know someone who killed himself?"

"Uh...no." Jake quickly regained his composure. "What happens at this place?"

"Punishment. The suicides have to work there. Very hard labor, from what they say. There are rumors of a revolt a few years ago-led by someone named Hemmings or Hemingway-and there are escape attempts. Some succeed, but eventually they're brought back by the apostles. Take Harriet for example."

"The woman I saw hiding outside your house."

"Yes. Harriet Westbrook, my first wife."

"Why was she yelling that way?"

"She killed herself when I left her for Mary Godwin. She shows up here on occasion, screaming, taunting...haunting me. If I could just talk to her...but I can never catch her. She runs from me. The apostles eventually show up and drag her back to the Isle of Labor, the poor soul."

Jake stared for a moment at Shelley. He was clearly upset. Did he still have feelings for the woman?

"What about Mary? Is she here, too?" Jake asked.

"I don't know. I've never looked for her." Now he really looked depressed.

"Why not? It's not like you don't have the time, or anything."

"The only way to travel here is by boat. It's something I just can't do." Shelley, visibly shaken, stood up and walked to the railing.

"Why can't you?" Jake pressed him.

"The sea killed me. That's how I got here. My friend, Edward Williams, and I were caught in a gale off the coast of Italy while sailing. The boat took on water and sank. I couldn't swim, but it would have mattered little in that violent sea. Dear Edward held onto me, trying to keep me above the water, but when I realized I was pulling both of us down I pushed him away. That's all I remember. When I awakened, I was in this house."

A tear ran down Shelley's cheek. He wiped it away. Jake stood and walked over to Percy. "It's okay, Man. It's okay," he said.

"Do you have any ghosts haunting you, Jake?" Shelley eyed him intently.

"I guess we all have ghosts we'll have to confront one day," Jake replied. "Where can I get a boat?"

Shelley looked back at the sea. "There's a dock on the other side of the island. You can get a small sloop there from a dockhand. He used to work on the Isle of Labor. It seems if you put in time and behave yourself there, you can get an easier job on one of the resident islands."

So there is a way to escape this place. "I'd go crazy if I had to stay on this rock for 200 years."

"Well, I've become friends with all my neighbors, so at least I have people to talk to. Albe came through and stayed awhile, too. He gave me some company."

"Who's Albe?"

"Lord Byron. George Gordon. He's a fellow poet. He stayed here with me for a couple of years. We wrote a little poetry and talked about old times. He tried to convince me to leave with him. He was looking for his sister. Probably still is..." Shelley stared out at the horizon.

"His sister?" Jake prompted.

"They were very close. There was quite a scandal back on Earth. He loved her dearly. A little too dearly, the rumors spoke."

"I see..." Jake said. "Maybe he'll be back."

"I don't think so," mumbled Shelley. "Do you think you'll get back, Jake?"

"Maybe I'm just having an after-life experience," Jake answered.

"Afterlife experience? What's that?"

"People have them all the time these days," Jake answered. "It's when you're dead for just a short time. You leave your body and go to Heaven or wherever and then you wake up soon after, good as new."

"Fascinating. I don't recall any of those in my time on

Earth," Shelley said. "When you wake up, you can tell the world about this place, and that you met the famous poet, Percy Shelley."

"Are you kidding? I have a reputation to protect. Besides, I'm already famous."

"Oh, you are? For what, may I ask?"

"Surfing."

"Yes, I remember that listed as your occupation in the register at the Inn. But what is 'surfing?'"

"You stand on a board riding on the ocean's waves," Jake said.

"Sounds silly. You were famous for that?"

"Don't knock it. It beats poetry any day."

"Don't be offended, my friend. I'd love to see you surfing and maybe you could read a little of my poetry."

"That reminds me, I need to go get my stuff. I hid a couple of boards and some clothes in the woods up the road from here."

"Your arrival package, I presume?"

"Huh?"

"When a person arrives he finds a few articles of clothing and some personal items. For you, that was your surfing boards."

"Surfboards," Jake corrected.

"When I arrived I found writing supplies."

"What happened when you ran out of paper?"

"I wrote on the walls. I wrote on the floor. And when the damned ink ran dry, I spilled by own blood and wrote with that," Shelley cried, waving his arms about madly.

Jake stared at him. "You're one weird guy, Percy."

Shelley only laughed and leaned far over the railing, as if ready to hurl himself over.

"Come on. Let's so get my stuff."

They both walked to the archway, through the curtains, and back into the house.

Chapter 7

They walked through the front room over a white tile floor and past the towering shelves of books. Jake saw the blue stones sitting on the reading table as he walked to the front door.

"Percy. What are those rocks for?"

"They provide light. Do you want to hold one?"

"I already have. C'mon, let's go."

Shelley shrugged as Jake opened the door. Both men were careful to look for any signs of the wayward apostles. When they agreed it was safe, they started up the path.

"Let's cut through the trees to be safe. We can shadow the path until we get to where my things are."

Shelley was walking quickly, almost running, to keep up with Jake.

"Yes, okay!" he said between breaths.

They continued on through the silent woods. Soon they were shadowing the main trail leading to Jake's house.

The sun peeped through the thick cover of oak and pine trees. A light breeze gently stirred the branches.

"Tell me Jake. What type of clothing is that?" Shelley was eyeing the wetsuit.

"It's called a wetsuit. It keeps you warm in the water."

"That keeps you warm? It looks about as thin as my knickers! How can that keep you warm?"

"It's made out of a special material."

"What? Seal skin?"

"No, you 19th-Century kook..."

They were now walking among waving palm and fruit trees and a few scattered pines.

"So there are no seagulls, squirrels, or birds. It's too quiet in these woods," Jake said.

"Not on this island or any other, except, maybe on the Lord's Isle."

"Lord's Isle?"

"He has to live somewhere doesn't he? The apostles say he has a great crystal palace there."

"The Emerald City," said Jake.

"Beg your pardon."

"Nothing. This is just like one big fairy tale, you know, like Alice in Wonderland."

"You mean Alice's Adventures in Wonderland. I have it back at the house!" Percy said merrily.

"I think you read too much, Percy. You need to get out more."

Shelley ignored the comment and kept walking.

"So what were your religious beliefs back on Earth, Percy?"

"I was an atheist," answered Shelley.

"An atheist!" Jake was alarmed. "Then why aren't you in..."

"I suppose my poetry brought enough joy to enough people to redeem me somewhat."

"But now you do believe..."

"No. I see a few men walking around preaching. Those in control never come out. Like back on Earth."

Jake was shocked. "But you've been here so long. You haven't aged. You've seen long dead friends and people from different time periods. What more proof do you need?"

"Just what is the proof and what does it really point to?" Shelley continued. "Who really is pulling the puppet strings in this place? I agree this place is extraordinary. Even Byron agreed with that. But who and what to believe...that is up to us."

Shelley reached down and picked up an oak leaf and then let it fall to the ground. "And where will we fall next time?" Shelley asked.

"So you're still an atheist?"

"I believe in a universal goodness. A supreme being... I'm not sure."

"Aren't you nervous about what'll happen to you, after you've been here 200 years, if you're still an unbeliever?"

Shelley laughed and patted Jake on the back.

"No more scared than back on Earth."

They came upon the spot where Jake had left the boards and clothing. Jake noticed several footprints. The palm branches had been removed and the clothing looked disturbed.

"The bastards took my sandals! They must have watched me hide the stuff. I knew I was being followed."

He grabbed up the remaining clothing and picked up a board under one arm. Shelley, likewise, picked up the other surfboard and they turned back toward Shelley's house.

"So this is a surfing board? It's quite heavy. You really stand upon this thing and ride through the water?"

"Sure do," Jake answered. "Let's cut over to the beach. We can walk back to your house that way. Maybe I can catch a set before dark."

"I don't understand," said Shelley.

"Come on, Percy. You want to see some surfing, don't you?"

Walking quickly through the forest they came upon the deserted, white-sand beach. The sun was still above the horizon on their backs. The water glimmered in the twilight and a soft wind blew in from the sea. They walked over the warm sand, leaving deep footprints in their wake. Smooth, glassy, six-foot waves were breaking in front of them. Jake could see Percy's house just up the beach.

Holding the surfboards, the two men stood at the ocean's edge-one ready to dash into the water, the other bewildered at the very idea of it. Jake looked over at Shelley. He looked as if he were in a trance as he stared out at the sea.

Chapter 8

To Jake Barr, it was just another ocean. Even after all he had seen and heard that day, he still couldn't let go of the passion that had always driven him.

"I think there's enough light for me to catch a couple. Percy you're about to see some surfing. Watch my clothes." Jake started wading into the water. "I'll be back in a few minutes."

"But it's getting dark! Those waters look dangerous!" Shelley was clearly agitated.

"Hey Percy, chill out, remember...I'm a professional."

"How does one chill out?"

"Just stay here. Yell and wave your arms if there's any trouble," said Jake.

Jake pushed his body onto the board and started out, leaving the confused Englishman behind. He dived under an incoming wave and looked back. Percy was still standing there with the second surfboard planted in the sand nearby. There was no sign of anyone else. The water felt warm and soothing. Jake sat up, straddling the board and looking for the next set. *This water doesn't feel like the ocean back in California. It's too clean. I can actually see the bottom.* Jake looked closely. *Are those some blue stones lying on the sand below?* He quickly looked up. A set was forming on the horizon. He angled his board toward the small, rising, blue hill and began to paddle. The wave picked him up as he stood, then down the face he glided. He quickly cut over, slashing up and down the steep wall of blue water. The wave was smooth and well formed. He turned back into the spray, reversing again as the crest of the wave spilled over him, finding himself in a perfect tube. He quickly came back out into the twilight, waving a fist in the air at Shelley who looked like he was dancing a jig on the sand. It was getting dark.

Jake rode the next wave into the shore. Percy came running up as Jake pulled himself onto the beach, water streaming from his mouth and nostrils.

"Neptune's Waltz!" Percy yelled.

"What?"

"You've inspired a poem," Percy said, his eyes merry.

"Hey man. It's just surfing. Don't go spilling your blood over it."

Shelley continued dancing his jig around Jake as they made their way back to Shelley's house.

The light was almost gone. They came to a flight of stairs leading up to the balcony, carefully laying the surfboards down and collapsing into the wooden chairs.

"That was the second most thrilling thing I've seen since I've been on this island," Shelley said.

"Second most? What was the other?"

"Byron's swim."

"Byron's swim?"

Shelley stood and walked over to the railing. The wind was blowing his curly locks around his eyes.

"Byron swam to the island you saw earlier." Shelley was pointing in the dark, out to sea. "And then he swam back."

"No way! That island must be at least five miles out there," Jake cried.

"Byron's an excellent swimmer! He swam the Hellespont, you know."

"The Hellespont?"

"Don't you modern men know anything? The Hellespont.

The channel in the Dardanelles." Shelley had a faraway look in his eyes. "Legends say Leander swam each night to see Hero, whom he loved. Hero would put a light in her tower at night to guide him. On one stormy night, the wind put out the light and Leander became lost and drowned. The next morning, Hero saw the body floating in the sea and in her grief she jumped into the sea and drowned herself."

"Bullshit!" Jake said.

"What do you mean, bullshit? Is there no romance or adventure in your time?"

"I get laid and I surf. That's all the romance and adventure I need," laughed Jake.

Shelley shook his head and mumbled something.

"Where is this hell point, anyway?" Jake asked.

"Hellespont!" Percy cried, "The Dardanelles, in the Turkish Empire. I believe the country is called Turkey in your day. How Albe hated those Turks!"

"Okay, if this is just some kind of afterlife experience and I do get back to Earth, I promise you I'll go to this Hellespont place and swim it."

"That's more like it. There's hope for you yet, Jake Barr. Now all I have to do is teach you how to write poetry."

"You're pushing it, Percy."

It had become pitch dark. The wind had picked up and was blowing across the balcony.

"I better bring us some light, my friend. I'll be right back." Shelley stood and slipped through the curtains, back into the house, leaving Jake alone.

Jake shivered. He was wet and cold. Perhaps Percy had a towel in there somewhere. It was so dark. There was no moon or stars. No lights were to be seen. A faint blue glow began to shine behind the curtains as Percy stepped through holding one of the blue stones. Shelley sat down and placed the stone on the ground between them filling the balcony with the soft glow. Jake felt a strange attraction to the rock and stared intently at it.

"What causes it to glow like that?" Jake asked.

"One of the many mysteries of this place," Shelley answered.

Jake looked up and said, "I can live here for 200 years and have a house of my own and surf everyday. No cares, no responsibilities-sounds like Heaven to me."

"It's incomplete though. There are pieces missing. You'll get tired of surfing. You'll miss food."

"Food. I haven't felt hungry and today's almost gone," Jake said.

"Exactly. No one has much of an appetite here. The fruit is all there is. Just one a day is all one really needs," said Shelley.

"I did eat one earlier."

"That's why you're not hungry. But you'll miss your leg of lamb, Christmas goose, and the rest. I was fortunate to have been a vegetarian, although a variety of fruit would've been nice," Shelley said.

"I guess I can live without meat," Jake responded.

"And without love?" Shelley said, serious looking.

"You mean without an old lady?"

"I mean, won't you miss having a woman in your life? You won't miss having a companion?" Shelley asked.

"I've got those two companions," Jake said, pointing at his surfboards.

"Barr, I do think you're hopeless!" Shelley's face showed a look of disgust in the light. Shelley stood and walked over to the rail, looking out towards the sea.

"Aren't there any women around here? I think I recall

reading some female names on those logs at the Inn," Jake said.

Shelley turned and looked at him.

"Do you really think the women you'll find here will be the pretty little dolls you can so easily use and discard at your whim like the ones you've been abusing back on Earth?"

"They're still women, aren't they? They still have needs, right? Maybe you and the rest of the kooks around here are just not man enough to meet those needs."

Shelley walked over to Jake. Jake stood up. They were inches apart.

"You have so much to learn, my arrogant friend, about life, about this place. Back on Earth, you..."

A shrill cry interrupted Shelley.

"Peerrccccy...Shheeelley! Percy!" The shouts came from down on the beach somewhere.

"It's Harriet! She's back! Hide!" Shelley cried.

"Tell her to go drown herself again," Jake said.

Shelley picked up the glowing stone and ran to the top of the stairs leading down to the sand.

"She'll keep doing this forever! I must catch her!" He ran down the stairs, leaving Jake in the dark.

Jake made his way over to the rail. He watched as the blue light bobbed and weaved down the beach towards his house.

"You're wasting your time on that crazy woman!" Jake cried out.

The blue light continued on down the beach and up towards the tree line.

A long row of torches glowed just offshore in front of Jake's house. Jake watched as the lights slowly approached his house. *Those must be boats.* The row of lights stopped momentarily and then started up the beach towards his house. He could make out many figures walking through the sand. It looked like about 50 individuals.

A rescue party! He ran over to the top of the stairs. The figures were now converging on his house. Some of the lights went up the stairs to his balcony as others moved in both directions around the house. Jake ran down the stairs and onto the cool sand. He could hear faint voices coming from the beach. He paused and listened. It sounded like orders being yelled out, "Find him," and "He's not here, Master!" Other voices began piercing the air from in and around Shelley's house.

"You three search this house! The rest of you form a line and walk towards Barr's house."

Jake crouched down in the sand. It was a trap. It must be the guys who jumped him earlier and now the survivor was back with help. Where was Shelley? He had to get to Percy before they got him. He rose and began to run down the beach.

A voice called softly but urgently from the trees just up the beach from Jake.

"Jake! Quickly come this way! Save yourself!" It was a woman's voice.

Jake looked in the direction of the voice. It was too dark to make out who it was. It might be that Harriet chick, and he wanted no part of her!

"Jake, I'm a friend. You must come with me or these evil men will kill you!" came the voice again. Jake took a few steps in the direction of the voice. More shouts came from Percy's house.

"He's not here!" A line of torches began to form outside Percy's house.

Jake ran towards the woods. A blurry but familiar looking form stood in the trees.

"Who are you?" asked Jake. "I have to find Shelley first."

"There's no time for Shelley!" the woman whispered urgently. "Quick. This way!" A soft but firm hand reached out and took his own, jerking him into the woods. He could hear voices behind.

"Fresh footprints! Here on the beach!"

The woman pulled him along quickly through the forest. Jake ran fast. It was all he could do to keep up with her and keep from stumbling. He wondered how she could see where she was going in the dark woods.

They came to a clearing. Jake could feel the grainy sand of a path beneath his feet. Torches were coming from the left along the path and among the trees near it.

"Back into the woods!" the woman whispered. She pulled Jake around and back into the trees.

"Get down!" She pulled him to the ground and flung a cloak over both of them, hugging her warm and perspiring body closely with his. Her body shook with heavy breaths. Jake could hear voices all around them passing them by.

"Keep your eyes open! We will drive him to the Master!"

Jake felt a leg brush against him but nothing happened. Soon the voices and footsteps grew faint.

"It's safe now. Let's go," the woman said.

Jake reluctantly got up as the woman led him across the path and into the forest on the other side.

A hand grabbed Jake by the hair and he felt the cold steel of a blade at his throat. A body pressed him from behind. He let go of the woman's hand.

"Oh, the Master will be pleased with me. You won't get away this time, Barr," his captor whispered in his ear.

Whoever it was had very bad breath. Jake had to do

something before this guy alerted the others. The hand around his throat squeezed tighter.

His captor was hit with a blow from behind, sending both of them tumbling into the dirt. Jake twisted around and managed to grab both of his attacker's hands. The knife was gone. He put one hand to the man's throat and ran the other over his head. It was bald. The man threw a punch, catching Jake in the cheek. Jake put both hands around the man's throat and squeezed. *This guy won't be screaming.* He held on till he could feel the tension leaving the man's body. Finally the man became very still, slumping against him and falling to the ground.

"You killed him. You have killed someone here," the woman's voice came from behind him.

"It was me or him. I chose him," Jake said.

They watched as the body glowed softly and then faded away.

"Come. We need to leave here. They may be back," the woman said.

She was once more pulling him through the dark silent woods. The silence was broken only by the sound of their feet breaking an occasional twig.

"Hey, lady, whatever your name is, thanks for hitting that guy from behind. Another second and I would've got it."

"What do you mean? I hid and watched you two fight," the woman replied as she pulled him along.

"Wait a minute. Someone hit him from behind. If it wasn't you, then who was it?"

"I don't know. Did you really have to kill him?"

"Hell yes, haven't you ever heard of self-defense?" Jake answered.

"It's only a little further now," the woman said.

They walked on for a few more minutes until they spoke again.

"It's just ahead now. We're almost there."

"Wha...what is?" Jake said, out of breath.

"My home."

Jake, still being led like a child, could see nothing. A tree branch smacked him in the face causing him to softly cuss.

The woman came to a stop.

"We had better sleep here for tonight. They may come and search my house, too. The house is just to your right."

Jake looked through the dark outlines of the trees. His eyes were just beginning to adjust to the darkness. Between two huge oaks he could barely make out the form of a rooftop.

A small blue stone began to glow in the woman's cupped hands. The light revealed an attractive dark face with large dark eyes and full lips. She had long, flowing brown hair that was somewhat unkempt, giving her a wild, alluring appearance.

"My name is Emily Adams."

"Jake Barr, glad to know you. You live over there?"

"Some of us live by the sea. Others, like myself, have forest homes."

"There's a house down by the ocean with my name on the door," Jake said.

"I found you floating in the sea this morning. I carried you up to your house and put you in your bed," Emily continued.

"So it was you. Why was I floating in the sea?"

"We all awake here in different spots, but always near our homes. I awoke lying in the grass. When I died here, I awoke safely in my bed," Emily said.

"You died here? How?"

"I climbed the tallest tree I could find the day after I got here. I wanted to see this place from up high. I slipped and fell. The next thing I remember was lying in my bed, good as new."

Jake scratched his head. "So we can die here and be right back where we started," Jake thought out loud.

The blue stone started to dim.

"It won't glow for much longer. It's a small stone," she said.

Jake looked closer at her. She was wrapped in a dark cloak and wearing a short leather dress.

"I wanted to see your face again, and I guess you wanted to see me also," she said, holding the light up between them.

"When did you get here, Emily?"

It was 1870. My family was traveling west to California. I was seventeen years old. I was going to meet my fiancé. He had made a fortune in gold out there. On the way, I caught fever and died. I've since found out my fiancé had already married another woman, even before we left for California."

"Jerk," said Jake.

"Funny," Emily said.

"What?"

Emily was staring intently at him. "You look just like him."

The remaining light of the blue stone began to fade away.

Chapter 9

A dark soul named Menon had invaded a place of balance- a Limbo where souls might mend or be broken forever. Menon's escapades on Earth had earned him a special place on the fringe of the deepest pit of Hell. During the seventh century he'd wandered Europe, killing indiscriminately. It was before the crimes of serial killers had actually been recorded, but during the Dark Ages not much of anything was recorded, except perhaps despair and suffering.

He'd been sent here on a mission to upset the balance. So far things were going as planned. He had the Angel of Limbo under his thumb and most of the apostles as well. Now a new presence had appeared: a counter to his evil.

He'd been warned to expect a fight, even a war, but not with just one man sent from Earth. The man's name was Jake Barr, and so far he was eluding his grasp. He would send the faceless one to find Barr. The creature had wings and would find Barr from above.

It was no former human, but something else Hell had invented to torture lost souls. Menon himself had been given back his youthful appearance. Back in Europe he'd lured many a peasant girl to her doom with this face.

The master would help him in his dreams. In the land of dreams he would find Jake Barr.

Jake paused at the side gate and looked back at the bicycle. He'd had one stolen and didn't want another one to disappear. He could hear the faint idle of a car engine nearby. A dog was howling from a nearby yard as if he were in great pain. Jake slowly opened the gate. The station wagon sat there waiting for him. The heat of the summer evening sent sweat running down his forehead. The howling dog was joined by another dog somewhere close by. Jake walked toward the idling auto, his heart beating loudly. He saw the red rag stuffed into the exhaust pipe. A figure was leaning against the glass on the driver's window. The window began to roll down. Jake froze.

"Jake," came a rasping voice from the car.

Jake didn't recognize the voice.

"Let me out, Jake. It's hard to breath in here son."

Jake took a step toward the car. The window rolled down further. Something hideous stared at him. It looked as though the very skin had been peeled from it's face.

"Come here you little brat and open this damn door!"

Jake turned to run.

Hands were upon him, shaking him from his stupor. Jake looked up and into Emily's face.

"Wake up, Jake. Are you okay?"

Jake set up in a small, grassy clearing surrounded by vine-laden, towering oaks. The sun was just up on the horizon, barely peeping through the forest at them.

"I'm okay. Just dreaming, I guess," Jake said.

Emily sat next to him, looking concerned.

"You're sweating. And you were talking in your sleep."

"I'll be okay. Any sign of the enemy?"

"Nothing. I've been walking around listening for them. It seems like they've left the island," Emily replied.

"We have to go back and find Shelley," Jake said. He stood and looked over at the house sitting a few yards away through the trees.

Emily rose to her feet.

"Maybe we should go and talk to the village seer."
"Who is that?" asked Jake.
"There is one in the village at the pools on every island. He grants one question to each visitor."
"You mean that crazy old man?"
"Yes," she laughed.
"What are all those birdbaths for at that place?"
"The pools are a form of entertainment here I guess. You can look into one and see anywhere on Earth or into Earth's past," Emily answered.
"Sounds kind of like television."
"That was after my time, youngster."
"First let's find Shelley," Jake said, taking her hand, "then we'll see the wizard."

Jake thought how pleasing Emily looked in the glowing daylight. Her long flowing hair danced around her bright brown eyes.

"I need to put my wrap in the house first," she said.

They walked over to her house.

The house had a small brown-frame with a red thatched roof. It had a fairy-tale air about it, like a place just waiting for Little Red Riding Hood. Jake read the plaque:

E. Adams
1853-1870

"You don't look 127 to me, Emily."
"Thanks," she laughed, opening the door and throwing the cloak somewhere inside.
"My house is a mess or I'd invite you in."

She closed the door and faced him. Standing there in her short leather skirt, Emily's figure was without flaws. Jake found himself staring at her.

"Are you okay, Jake?"

"Yeah. Sorry. Let's go find Percy."

A dark shape flew over them.

"Don't move," she whispered.

The flying creature passed over and out of sight.

"Quick! Into the woods!" Jake said. He grabbed her and they ran into the trees and crouched down.

The creature flew back into range at a lower altitude. It stopped and hovered above Emily's cottage, slowly descending until it sat on the roof, and peered down at the front door. To Jake it looked like a gargoyle—half-man, half-demon sitting there.

The creature fell off the roof and hit the ground with a thud. Emily let out a small gasp. Jake quickly put his hand over her mouth. The monster hadn't heard her. It was looking around on the ground near the door as if searching for clues. It looked at the door sign. A clawed hand rose and turned the doorknob of Emily's front door. The door pushed inward and the creature disappeared into Emily's house.

"Come on. Let's go while it's inside!" Jake whispered.

"But I don't want that in my house!"

He pulled her away and they started to run.

They stopped several yards away, crouching down and listening.

A loud roar sounded from Emily's house. Then the monster flew over them and disappeared through the trees.

Chapter 10

Jake and Emily made their way through the silent forest. They stopped to listen for the creature. There was no sign of it or the baldies.

"Last night the apostles kept saying something about the master. Who do you think they were talking about?" Jake asked as they walked.

"I don't know. The only ruler here is the Angel of Madness," she answered.

"You mean the Lord of Limbo?" Jake asked.

"And when you say the apostles, do you mean the messengers of the Angel?" Emily asked.

"God, can't anyone agree on anything around here?"

They came to the main path that ran on the coast around the island. Jake looked down the path in both directions. It was clear. They crossed into the trees onto the other side.

"Which way to Percy's house?" Jake asked.

"It's just ahead to the right."

They came into a clearing.

What was left of Shelley's house stood in front of them. A trail of smoke drifted skyward from the caved in roof. Dark smears of soot left a stain from the front window. There was no sign of life anywhere. Jake ran towards the house.

"Jake! Wait it could be a trap!" Emily cried.

"Percy could be in there," Jake shouted. "Stay there!"

Jake pulled open the front door. A wall of heat and smoke poured over him. He plunged into the house. Percy's books were burning in a large pile in the middle of the room. The shelves were engulfed in flames, spreading up to the roof which had collapsed above. Beams and blue tiles spilled down to the floor. The two reading chairs, the table and the remains of a surfboard burned on the pyre.

"Damn them!" Jake yelled.

Jake ran into the bedroom. The bed was engulfed in flames. There was no sign of anyone. He ran back into the sitting room and out through the burning curtains to the balcony. The other surfboard lay there, broken in two.

"You bastards!" Jake screamed into the morning.

Emily came up the stairway from the beach.

"Did you find him?"

"No. Look what they did to my boards!"

"But, that's just a piece of wood. Why are you upset?"

"I can't live without that," Jake said.

Emily was now looking down the beach.

"Jake..."

Jake followed Emily's eyes down the beach. There were plumes of smoke coming from his house as well.

"Maybe Percy's there. Come on!" They ran down the stairs to the sand. The sun was just above the horizon, tickling the sea.

⁂

It sat in an oak tree, watching the two humans running exposed along the beach. They would be easy prey there. Neither carried a weapon or had cover to hide behind. There was no need to rush things-play with the mouse awhile and then finish the business. It would wait. Let them reach the other house. They could be cornered there easily. It would kill the woman and take the man back alive.

⁂

Jake opened the front door, shielding his face from the heat. Smoke poured out, pushing him back.

"Percy! Are you in there?" He walked back to the side of the house, noticing several footprints nearby. Something got his attention on the lower wall. Emily joined him.

"Find anything?" she asked.

"Yes." He pointed to the message written in blood on the wall:

said u left island
P S

"He must be alive," said Emily.

"Why take him with them?" Jake questioned. "Let's go to the village. I want to talk to that old man."

They started walking toward the woods. Something shot from a tree and began flying at them. Jake saw the creature and put his body in front of Emily. They both fell to one knee as the monster swooped low in its first pass. They rose and began running for the trees. The creature landed in front of them, blocking the way. It stood nearly five feet tall, and was very stout and thick limbed. It had a gray, stony body. Large gray wings closed behind it. It smiled a face that held too many teeth. Two black marbles stared out at them. It began walking towards them with two clawed hands reaching out.

"When I say run, you run," Jake whispered.

"I want to stay with you, Jake," she whispered back, gripping his hand.

The creature stopped. A strange look came over its face, as if it were suddenly confused. It fell over, landing on its face in front of them, an arrow stuck from its back.

"My God!" Emily cried.

Jake walked slowly over to the creature's side. He kicked it hard in the ribs. It didn't flinch. He looked up into the trees. No one walked out to claim the good shot. He looked back down at the corpse. He stooped and pulled the arrow out of the creature's back. Green ooze flowed from the wound.

"Yuck," Emily said.

"The arrowhead is carved from one of those blue stones," Jake said, holding the arrow skyward.

"Singing Wind," Emily said.

Chapter 11

"Singing Wind?" Jake repeated.

"An Indian. He lives on the other side of the island. He keeps mostly to himself."

"Why would he want to help us?" Jake asked.

Emily shrugged and looked toward the woods.

"Singing Wind!" she yelled. The woods remained still. "He's on the shy side. My father always said there were no good Indians. I never believed him."

"Well this guy's pretty good with the bow. C'mon, let's go to the village."

They disappeared into the cover of the trees, and soon came upon a small pond. Jake walked to the edge of the water and peered down. The water was very clear. He could see a layer of waving foliage deep below.

"Tell me, Emily," Jake said, as he stared into the clear blue water, "Why are you here?"

When she didn't answer, he looked up. She had stripped out of the dress and was standing a few feet away at the edge of the pond. She was unabashed in her nakedness. Her body was slim and supple with full round breasts. Jake was both thrilled and surprised.

Emily knelt down and splashed water onto her face. She looked up and smiled at Jake, who quickly turned away as if he'd seen the Virgin Mary herself.

"You did think we took baths here, didn't you?" She stood and dived into the pond, coming up several yards away. Her soaked breasts were half exposed to the rising sun. She flung her hair back with a quick movement and swam a little toward Jake.

"Jump in."

"Nah, I'm fine." He crouched down in the grass, hiding his excitement.

Emily swam over and pulled her body out and onto the grass. She grabbed the skirt and slipped it over her body. "I used to be afraid to come to these ponds. I'd bathe only at night. Time erased those inhibitions."

Jake stood and walked over to her.

"So everyone's one big happy family here. Orgies at Percy's every Friday night too?" Jake said.

Emily reached out and slapped him, surprising him. She started walking away.

"Hey! Wait up. I didn't mean anything!" He caught up with her.

"Sex is forbidden here," she said, looking down as she walked. Her hair was now in thick tangled heaps.

"You act like a child, Jake."

"No. There's something else bothering you. What is it?" He jumped in front of her and grabbed her by the shoulders. "You can tell me, Emily."

Wounded she looked up and gazed into eyes that were ready to accept.

"I am doomed, just like you, Jake," she said at last.

"I don't understand."

"You killed a man here," she said, "and I had sex."

"With who? Who did you have sex with?"

"It was a long time ago. It was a visitor. His name was George, one of Percy's friends. He seduced me."

"Oh no," Jake mumbled to himself.

"You know him?" Emily asked.

"I know of him-the sister lover. Forget it. Did you love him?"

"No. It was nothing. He's probably seduced thousands of women here."

Jake noticed a tear rolling down her cheek. He reached over put an arm around her shoulder. "I don't think you're doomed, Emily."

A slight wind blew through the oak trees, stirring the hanging vines. Jake heard a small metal tinkling noise. There was a quick whooshing sound. Leaves flew all around. Jake felt his body being carried upward, enclosed by thick vines. Emily's body crushed up against him. They were trapped in a basket made of vines, suspended in the air. They bounced for a moment and then swung slightly in the breeze.

"What the hell!" Jake shouted.

"Jake!" Emily cried.

There was no movement from the surrounding trees. Jake heard something rustle nearby in the undergrowth. A wiry man emerged from the shadows. He was wearing a camouflage uniform and a helmet. He had sandals on his feet and carried a spear in one hand. He crept closer and stared at his captives. Jake could make out the words "Born Killer," painted on the helmet. A pair of dog-tags swung from his neck.

"That you, Emily?" the man asked in a low squeaky voice, aiming the spear at her rump.

"Hey! Watch it with the spear man!" Jake shouted.

"Who we got here? Who is he Emily?" the man's voice was louder, with a nervousness to it.

"Newt! It's okay. He's a friend!" Emily cried.

"You don't know that. He could be one of *them*." The man was now giving Jake the spear's attention.

"No Newt, really. He's an American, just like you. Please let us down."

"Who is this psycho?" Jake whispered.

"His name is Newt Worley. He..."

The point of the spear touched Jake's underside.

"Ouch! Watch it asshole!" he shouted.

"Charlie's got his shit together here, Emily. That blonde hair don't mean nothin'. Could be a Ruskie."

"What?" Jake asked.

"You shut up. I'm askin' the questions here," Newt said.

"What year is it?"

"1997, on Earth," Jake answered.

"Ha! That's a good one. Can't be no later than 1970. What's the Beatle's drummer's name?"

"Ringo."

"The President's nickname?"

"Slick Willie."

"Wrong! Tricky Dick, you commie bastard!" Newt ran up behind the trapped pair, pulling out a wad of vine rope. Jake felt his wrists being tied.

"Hey!" Jake cried. He was handcuffed.

"Newt! His name is Jake Barr! He's from California. He's a surfer!"

Newt reached up and cut the vines supporting the trap. Jake and Emily spilled out onto the ground. Newt looked them in the eyes.

"Charlie don't surf! Get up!" The spear was pointed at Jake.

Emily and Jake stood. Jake tried to loosen the vines from around his wrists.

"Turn around and start walking. Emily, you git. I'm takin' him back."

"I'm staying with him, Newt."

"Suit yourself, but it ain't gonna be pretty," Newt said.

"Where do you think we are man?" Jake asked.

"You know where this is! It's God-damn Vietnam! This is a communist re-education camp! Don't you play stupid with me! Now start walking!" Newt pointed the spear at Jake's mid-section. Jake turned and started walking, Emily at his side. Newt followed closely behind.

"Dude. The Vietnam War ended over twenty years ago. You're living in a dreamworld."

"Oh yeah, and who won?" Newt asked.

"America lost."

"Shut your mouth! America don't lose no wars!"

Jake felt the point of the spear press into the wetsuit on his back.

"Jake is telling the truth Newt. He really is an American. A surfer from California." Emily looked over at Jake and shrugged. "I read your entry at the Inn. I don't know what a surfer is."

"I have a test for our friend when we get to my pad," Newt said. "We'll see if he's tellin' the truth."

Chapter 12

They came to a clearing surrounded by tall oaks and scattered pines. A forest home stood in the middle.

Jake walked to the front door and stopped. He glanced at the door, looking for the occupant sign. It had been torn away. Someone had carved, "Better dead than red," on the door. *He got his wish.*

"Emily, you open the door and get him in there. Nothing funny now," Newt said.

Emily opened the door and walked in, followed by Jake and Newt. In the middle of the room a man sat strapped to a chair. He was oriental-looking and appeared to be distraught. He flashed wild eyes at the threesome.

"Nguyen!" Emily cried.

"Don't talk to the prisoner, Emily. He's certified Viet-Cong."

"Him crazy!" the restrained man yelled.

"You shut up, Charlie!" Newt walked up and slapped the man across the head. The fellow moaned and shook his head.

"You know this guy, Emily?"

"His name is Nguyen Van Phu. He lives on this island. At least he used to. He disappeared some time ago. I just thought he'd left the island."

"Me been here. He keep me here." Nguyen moaned.

"I told you to keep quiet." Newt raised the spear.

"Hey, give the guy a break," Jake said.

"Yeah, like they gave my buddies a break in the jungle!" Newt shouted.

Jake looked around the room. There was the same wall of books on one side. Besides Nguyen in his solitary chair, a pile of wood and vines sat nearby. Jake looked over at the archway that led out to a small patio. Seven black robes hung from the archway. No white curtains blew in the wind there. Newt noticed Jake's stare.

"I got them bald gooks. They tried to brainwash me with their propaganda."

"You killed the Angel's messengers?" Emily said.

"Poor Emily," Newt said, looking at Jake. "They really got her mind messed up good."

"Newt, why don't you just let Jake and Nguyen go? No one wants to hurt you."

"I thought you said you had a test for me. A way I could prove I'm American," Jake said.

"That's right. I do. Get on into the bedroom. Door to the left there."

Jake walked ahead of Newt. Upon entering the bedroom he was amazed to see a twenty-foot-long wooden board lying next to the unmade bed.

"Pick it up," Newt said.

"Are you going to untie me first?"

"No funny stuff." Newt cut the vines away with the spear.

"You surf?" Jake asked. The board was very heavy.

"Sure do. I picked it up here in the Nam from a grunt from California named Kelly. He looked kinda like you. C'mon, let's go."

"Where?"

"The beach."

They heard a commotion in the front room. Newt ran out. Jake lumbered behind, hauling the heavy, oak board.

Nguyen was gone.

"He got away," Emily said, trying to look innocent.

"Damn! And he was about to crack too!" Newt ran to the open front door. "He's long gone. You didn't help him did you?" Newt eyed Emily suspiciously.

"Why no. I wouldn't help the enemy," Emily answered, winking at Jake.

"Well I still got this one. Outside. Let's go." Newt ushered them out the door and into the midday sun. "That way," Newt said, pointing at a spot in the woods.

They walked between two thick pines. Jake stopped. Standing before him, hidden in the trees stood a small airstrip. The balloon rose almost as high as the massive oaks around it. Clothes of all sorts and eras were patched together giving the balloon a colorful, abstract appearance. There were petticoats, togas, dinner jackets, and blue jeans to name a few. A small basket made from thickly woven vines hung below. The balloon was held in place with vines tied to nearby trees. Jake could see an uneven, patchy tube running from the basket back to the rear of the house. He figured that was where the heat was coming from.

"My goodness," Emily said. "It's a flying machine."

"Gonna float over the Pacific back to the States, or at least the Philippines," Newt said. "You've seen how I'll escape. You better know how to surf, Jake Barr, or whatever your name is."

They walked on past the balloon and headed for the ocean. As Jake toiled under the load of the long board, he spied the face of a man peering out from behind some nearby brush. The man had long dark hair. As quick as the face appeared, it vanished. They were being followed.

Chapter 13

Jake and Emily walked out of the woods and onto the beginning of the beach. Newt followed behind.

"Newt, why don't you just go get a boat and leave. What's with the balloon?" Jake asked.

"You kiddin'? There's Cong patrol boats out there in the water."

The wide, blue sea opened up before them. Waves were breaking just off shore. They appeared to be about three to four feet in height. Jake was relieved. He didn't have much experience with these boards, especially with larger waves.

The weight of the board drove Jake's feet deep into the hot sand, now blistering under the noonday sun.

"Keep walkin', down to the surf," Newt said.

The sea was soon lapping at their feet, giving relief from the heat. Jake set the board in the water, waded out a little and looked back. Newt stood there holding the spear, pointing it at Emily.

"No funny stuff or Emily here gets it!"

Jake lifted himself up and lay on the board. He struggled to paddle the mammoth creation out of the shore break. The surface of the board was chipped and coarse, as if it had been recently hacked out of a tree. He looked back at the beach. Emily and Newt stood there watching patiently. The water felt perfect—just slightly warm, as it splashed around him. Newt was definitely deluded, and there was no telling what he would do if Jake didn't play along. He would simply ride this board in and then he and Emily would be on their way.

There was a slight rising in the ocean before him. Jake struggled to turn. He was sideways as the wave lifted the board. He found himself being toppled over into the wave as it broke around him, driving him just under the surface of the sea. He held his breath and swam upward, breaking the surface, and looking for the board. Laughter came from the beach.

"You stupid commie!" Newt yelled.

"Jake, be careful!" Emily cried.

Jake spied the board floating nearby. He swam over and climbed back aboard. He looked back at the beach, half expecting to see the spear being hurled in his direction. Emily waved. Jake waved back. Newt was standing beside her with arms stretched out. His body was in a crouch as if riding an imaginary surfboard. Emily must have asked Newt what surfing was all about. Jake looked back at the horizon. Another set was forming.

Jake paddled the board into position. He'd be ready this time. The first wave picked him up. He paddled with deep, determined strokes, but the wave came and went on by, leaving him behind eating its spray. The second wave slowly lifted the great board up, and with one determined kick, Jake stood and rode down the small face. The board needed a little steering. Being so heavy, it cut deeply into the small wave and labored over to the shoulder and glided towards the shore. The wave fizzled out as Jake jumped off into the shore break, pulling the board on to shore.

"You call that surfin'?" Newt said, running up, helmet tilted back. Emily was right behind him.

"I'm a short board rider. I don't fool with these dinosaurs too much," Jake responded.

"Is that right?" Newt asked thoughtfully. "I guess you passed. Here, I'll carry it back. You take this." Newt gave Jake the wooden spear and took the long board from him.

They began walking up the beach towards the trees.

"Now what unit were you with before the commies put you on this rock?" queried Newt.

"Uhh, the 11th," Jake said. He winked at Emily. She smiled back.

"The 11th? Never heard of 'em. Area of operations?" Newt asked, as they reentered the forest.

"Saigon. We were a small Army outfit," Jake answered. This was getting tricky. He'd better put Newt on the defensive before these questions got out of hand.

"Newt. How did you get here? How were you captured?" Jake asked. Jake caught a movement nearby in the trees. Someone was still following them.

"That's the funny part. I don't remember a damn thing," Newt said, tilting his helmet back. "I was with the Delta Company, up in Hue. Charlie had his shit together there, man. He gave that city the shits! We were takin' it from all sides. A nice damn city, Hue."

"What happened?" Jake asked.

"I was with three other guys-Robinson, Greer and Rodriguez. Our squad was in a hell of a firefight. All three of my buddies got hit. Next thing I knew I was here. I must of got knocked out and taken to this place," Newt said. "I figure we're somewhere off the coast of North Vietnam."

An arrow whizzed from nowhere, thudding into the side of the long board, which Newt promptly dropped.

"Oh shit!" Newt cried.

Another arrow flew in, cutting through the sleeve of Newt's camouflage jacket, pinning him to a tree. Jake and Emily stood there in shock.

A figure ran out of the trees and came toward them. It was a dark, well-toned man, wearing nothing but a leather loincloth around his waist. He carried a shoddy, wooden bow in one hand and a small dagger in the other hand. Hanging from the man's shoulder was a sling-like quiver full of arrows.

The man ran up and stood in front of Newt, who stared out defiantly.

"Singing Wind!" Emily said.

"You owe me," said the stranger, to Newt.

"I think we're even now, red man," Newt answered.

"I give you arrowheads. You give back."

"Okay. Get me loose. You come by the house tonight and get what you want," Newt said.

The stranger reached out and plucked the arrow out of Newt's jacket, freeing him from his impaling.

"I will be there when the sun sleeps. Be ready," the man said, turning and running into the brush and out of sight.

"Damn him," Newt said, brushing his jacket.

"So that's Singing Wind?" Jake said.

"Yes," Emily said.

Newt growled.

"What does he want with you?" Jake asked.

"I trade for his arrowheads," Newt said.

"And what did you give him?" Emily asked.

"Stick around, and you'll find out tonight," Newt said.

They continued walking back to Newt's house. This time they didn't walk past the balloon, but came out in a different area of the clearing surrounding Newt's home. Newt took the board inside, leaving Jake and Emily outside.

"We could leave him now, you know," Emily said.

"The guy's kooky, but I like him for some reason," said Jake. "It's not everyday you meet someone trapped in the sixties."

"The 1960's. What was so special about those years?" asked Emily.

"It was a time when people weren't afraid to try or think anything. A lot of people began to loosen up."

"Hmmm...sounds like some of what I heard about the West from my fiancé's letters," Emily replied.

Newt stepped out the front door.

"So Jake, you better hang out here. There's a lot of gooks running around this place," Newt said.

"Me and Emily are heading to the village. We're going to talk to the old man," Jake said.

"Are you crazy? That's the head commissar himself! You want your brain drained or something?"

Jake handed the spear back to Newt.

"If you come with us I'm sure he won't try anything, Newt," Jake answered.

"I don't know man. I get a feeling this will be bad, just like at Hue."

"Have you been there before?" Jake asked.

"Yeah. I've taken some clothes from there, but don't think I don't check 'em for bugs!" Newt yelped.

Jake laughed and looked at Emily, who looked puzzled.

"There are no insects here, Newt," said Emily.

"C'mon you two. Which way to the village?" Jake said.

Newt walked toward the woods, spear thrust out. "Follow me," he said. Jake and Emily fell in behind him.

Chapter 14

Newt was the point man. He scouted ahead, stopping at times, arms raised, signaling Jake and Emily to get down. He smelled an ambush. After sitting in silence a few seconds, the arm would wave again. Jake and Emily walked several yards behind, talking quietly as the sunlight filtered down through the waving palms and mighty oaks.

"Newt said you were messed up in the head. What did he mean?" Jake asked.

"He thinks I'm part of his war, like he does you. When I ran into him for the first time, several years ago, he asked me those same questions. When I said Ulysses Grant was the last President I could remember, he was convinced I'd gone insane. He thinks I'm an army nurse that was captured by the enemy. I'd never even heard of the place called Vietnam."

"I guess we should just keep playing, until we get off this island."

"You think we should leave?"

"We're just targets here for whoever burned those houses or sent that flying thing after us. The quicker we leave, the better," answered Jake.

"Have you thought about your question?" asked Emily.

"No, not really." Jake was a little embarrassed. He knew how important this was not to ignore. "I've got to ask something that doesn't let the old man off with a short answer. What did you ask him? Have you ever asked him?"

"Yes. I asked him a question," she answered.

"What? Do I have to beg you to tell me?"

"I'll tell you later. It's personal."

"Just like a woman. You've been here over a hundred years and you're still playing games," Jake laughed.

"Shh...you two keep quiet back there. We're here," Newt whispered urgently. A building came into view up ahead. Newt ran to the back of the structure and planted his back against a wall. Jake and Emily walked up to the edge of the woods watching the paranoid Newt as he peeped around the corner of the building. Jake took Emily's hand and they walked up and stood by Newt.

Newt turned around.

"Holy Jesus! Don't sneak up on me," Newt whispered, raising his spear. "There's someone sittin' over there at a table, but she looks harmless." Emily looked in the direction of the café.

"That's just Olga," Emily said.

"That's a Russian name," Newt said.

"I'll vouch for her. She's a friend."

"All right," Newt said reluctantly. "Let's go."

Newt went around to the front of the building called, *Books*.

Jake and Emily followed.

"Hello Olga," Emily waved.

The blonde woman sitting alone at the café waved back.

"Hello Emily," she responded.

"Shh...why you wanna tell everybody we're here," Newt said, a little pissed off.

"C'mon man, it's just a lady sitting there," said Jake.

"Charles got his shit together here, Jake. You can't trust anybody." Newt looked around nervously, pulling his helmet up which had fallen down over his eyes. "Man, I gotta bad feelin' about this place."

Jake looked around the village. The lady sitting at the café was the only sign of life. He watched as Newt ran across one of the brick roads leading into the crossroad in the middle. Newt had run over to the pools, slamming his back against the wall next to the entrance. Newt then signaled Jake and Emily to join him. The woman sitting at the café watched curiously.

"Shall we join him?" said Jake.

"If we must."

They ran side by side over to Newt.

"Okay, I'll go in first," said Newt excitedly. "You two come in and cover my rear."

"How about if we just knock and walk in like normal human beings?" Jake said.

"Are you kiddin'? This place is liable to be booby trapped," said Newt.

"Listen private, I was a lieutenant in the war. We'll do it my way. Any problem with that?"

"Oh, no sir, none at all sir!"

"Okay. You were a private? Right?" queried Jake.

"Yeah, that's right," Newt responded, standing a little straighter, as though at attention.

Emily suppressed a giggle.

Jake stepped up to the door, knocked once, and pushed the heavy, wooden door open. He stepped upon the white marble floor and walked in. Emily followed. Newt came in next, walking backwards to guard their rear. Jake could see several of the birdbath-like fountains spread across the floor. A familiar figure approached from the corner of the dimly lit room.

"Ahh, you've come back Mr. Barr, and you've brought some friends," said the old man. "Mr. Worley, now he's a special case."

Newt spun around.

"You stay away from me! I know what you're up to!" Newt cried.

"Chill, Newt," Jake said. "I'm here to ask you my question." Emily looked at Jake expectantly.

The old man, as if puzzled, ran a wrinkled hand down his long beard that fell upon his feet.

"And what would that be young man?"

"Why am I here before my time?"

The old man pulled his white robe tight around his body as if he'd suddenly caught a chill. His head tilted back and he stared at the ceiling. He then let out a hysterical shrill of laughter that vibrated the room. Jake, Emily and Newt all stepped back.

"He's possessed by the Angel now," Emily said.

"What?" Jake said.

"Shhh, he speaks," she continued.

"A great evil sent from the bowels of hell itself has entered this realm. This demon is here to push Limbo into the grip of evil away from the neutral sea. You, Jake Barr, are here to stop him. You are divine intervention. Go forth and stop him. His name is Menon. He awaits you." The old man tilted his head back and let out another blast of insane cackles. He then looked back upon them. "Who's next?" he said calmly.

"Is that it?" Jake said. "Divine intervention? What's that supposed to mean?"

"Only one question per island, sorry. Who would like to see their death? You have two deaths, Jake Barr, but I can only show you the first one."

"How long do we have to stand here and listen to this commie bullshit?" Newt screeched.

"Jake, perhaps we should go now," Emily said, tugging on Jake's arm.

The old man walked over to one of the stone fountains.

"Come my friends, and look back on Earth."

Jake and Emily walked slowly over and stood by the fountain. Jake gazed down into the crystal-clear water just a few inches deep. Newt came up behind the pair and peered over Jake's shoulder. The water in the fountain began to get cloudy. The mist turned dark and began to swirl into a whirlpool. The water suddenly went flat and became a picture. Jake could see himself paddling on his surfboard. There was Charlie behind him. Charlie seemed to be yelling something at him but he just kept paddling. A large set of waves formed and Charlie took off on the first one. Jake watched himself catch the next wave and float down the fifteen-foot-wall of ocean. The Jake in the fountain did a bottom turn and then disappeared inside a massive barrel as the wave poured over him. He never came out.

"Now, Mr. Worley," the old man said.

"That was it? That's how I got here? I always dreamed of going that way, but not on a fifteen-footer," Jake said softly. "A thirty-footer at Waimea Bay was more what I had in mind."

"You wanted to drown?" Emily said.

"No, not suicide or anything like that," answered Jake.

"Now Mr. Worley, please step up. You've been here twenty-seven years. It's time you saw your death," the old fellow persisted.

"Maybe he shouldn't," said Jake.

"Nonsense! Look Mr. Worley!"

Newt stepped up between Jake and Emily. The ocean scene in the fountain had turned once again to the swirling dark mists and then gave way to a charred, city street. Four men crouched down in the street, surrounded by debris and litter. Flames poured from the surrounding buildings. It was a scene from Hell.

Newt almost stuck his head into the water.

"That's Robinson! Greer and Rodriguez!" Newt shouted.

The four grunts ran a few paces and then crouched down again. Three of the soldiers stood and walked a few steps down the road, shadowing a smoking ruin off to the side. Jake recognized the soldier in the rear as Newt. One of the men stopped and waved for Newt to come forward. Newt didn't move. The other two had also turned and all three were lip-syncing shouts at Newt.

"This can't be happenin'," said Newt, as he watched the drama in front of him, "this is some kinda trick."

Jake saw a small round object come rolling from a nearby doorway and roll directly behind the feet of Robinson, Greer and Rodriguez. The Newt in the fountain waved his arms, trying to warn his comrades of the grenade. The three soldiers kept shouting. Newt turned and ran as the explosion erupted behind him. Emily pulled closer to Jake, holding him for protection as though the scene might spill from the pool. Jake and Emily watched as a figure in black emerged quickly from the doorway, an AK47 in tow. The man positioned himself and sprayed the fleeing Newt in the back with several rounds.

"I hope I have been of service," said the old man.

"Aeeeeiiiii!" Newt screamed, raising his hands and beating himself about the "Born to Kill" helmet. "I was gonna jump on that grenade," he proclaimed nervously. "Honest Lt. Barr, I was gonna jump on it." Newt turned and ran screaming out the door and into the afternoon sunlight.

"Such are the demons of Purgatory," the old man said, stroking his beard.

Chapter 15

In the growing darkness, Jake and Emily made their way back to Newt's house. They found Newt curled up into a fetal position in his bed, his helmet resting beside him.

Newt looked up at Jake and Emily, who were standing in his bedroom doorway. A blue stone glowed next to the helmet, providing the house with a little light.

"Why don't you just leave me alone, surfer boy," Newt mumbled. Newt rose and walked toward Jake. "Just get the hell out of here!"

Jake stood still.

Newt started to cry, collapsing into Jake.

"Am I in Hell? Am I being punished?" Newt sobbed. "I didn't want my buddies to die."

Jake and Emily put their hands on Newt, trying to comfort him.

"It's okay, Newt. You're not being punished. There was nothing you could do for your friends," said Jake.

"You think I'm a coward. Don't you?" Newt cried.

"No, I don't think that," Jake answered.

"Neither do I," said Emily.

Jake looked at Newt's closely shaved, military style haircut. Newt's face was gaunt with deep-set eyes. His tall, thin body looked like that of a concentration camp survivor.

"Lt. Barr?"

"What?"

"Am I gonna get court-martialed?"

"How? This is not Vietnam, Newt. You're in Limbo or

Purgatory. For all I know, you're not here because of your actions in the war," said Jake.

"Them men I killed here. The bald men. What about them? I thought they were damn commies!"

Jake looked at Emily who could only shrug her shoulders.

"I don't know Newt. I don't know," Jake answered.

"I'm a damn mass-murderer here in the after-life." Newt walked back over and sat on the bed. He picked up his helmet and slung it against a wall.

"Maybe we should leave," Emily whispered.

"Wait," Jake said. Jake walked over and kneeled beside Newt.

"The men in black were once good men in this place. Now they are evil and have to be stopped. The ones you killed were probably evil-just like commies." Jake looked over and winked at Emily. "They work for the Devil now. You can join us and stop them, Newt."

"You mean it was a good thing I killed 'em?"

"That's right buddy. It was you or them-just like back in Nam."

Newt stood up and grabbed his spear off the floor.

"What are we waitin' for then? Let's go kill us some gooks!" Newt yelled.

"Same old Newt," Emily laughed.

There was a knock at the front door.

"It's them!" Newt hollered, running out the bedroom door past Jake and kicking Emily aside.

Jake and Emily followed after Newt who had taken up position next to the front door.

"Who is it?" Newt muttered.

"It's me, Singing Wind. I've come to collect," said a voice outside.

"What's the password?" Newt continued.

"Oh Newt, don't be silly. That's Singing Wind." Emily said.

"Howdy Doody," said the voice.

"Them boys in black can be tricky," Newt said, as he cracked the door open. He pulled it open and let Singing Wind enter. He was carrying an object wrapped in palm branches crisscrossed with vines.

"Whatcha got there, Speedy," said Newt.

"Gift, for the stranger," Singing Wind answered.

Jake could tell it had the shape of a surfboard.

Singing Wind walked over to Jake, carrying the "gift" longways out front, almost leveling Newt.

"You take this to the great river, One Who Walks on Water. You wait and open when you get there. You go now."

Singing Wind handed the package off to Jake. It felt like a board, not too heavy.

"Is that a surfboard? You crazy Indian, Jake can't surf in the dark," Newt said.

Singing Wind took a small stone out of a pouch that hung from his waist and gave it to Emily.

"This enough light to get you there," Singing Wind said. "Now you give me, Newt.

"Okay, okay. Don't rush me." Newt looked up at the wall of books. Which one?"

"Same."

Newt reached up and pulled a book down. "He likes this one. Last of the Mohicans, by James Cooper. I'm sick of it myself."

The blue stone began to glow in Emily's hand.

"We'll just go walk to the beach," Jake said. "Sound okay to you, Emily?"

"I guess," Emily said shyly.

Newt and Singing Wind had sat down on the floor. Newt reached over and pulled a blue stone from the lowest bookshelf. He opened the book and began to read: "It was a feature peculiar to the Colonial wars of North America, that the toils of danger of the wilderness..."

Jake and Emily edged over to the front door.

"Do you think it's safe?" she asked him.

"You're with Jake Barr. Would you rather stay and listen to story hour?" Jake opened the front door. It was solid black outside. They stood at the doorway, the blue stone lighting up the grass around the entrance.

"We'll be back," Jake said. But Newt only read on to Singing Wind, who sat with his legs crossed, listening attentively.

"Winding its way among countless islands and imbedded in mountains, the 'holy lake' extended a dozen leagues still further to the south..." Newt read on.

"Come on, looks like they're having too much fun," said Jake, tucking the concealed board under one arm and taking Emily's hand with his free hand. Emily pulled the door closed behind them.

꜀

This time they took a path to the sea. Circling the house they found the trail leading to the main road which circled the island. The blue light played with the shadows among the trees on both sides of the path. The trees towering over them gave off an eerie glow.

"So, Singing Wind carves things for Newt out of the blue stones, and in return Newt reads to him," Jake said.

"Apparently," Emily responded. "Maybe someone should teach Singing Wind how to read."

"I don't think Newt would like that too much."

A warm breeze began to move the tree branches back and forth in the soft blue light. *Emily looks beautiful, but sad. She's been marooned here for over a hundred years with maybe only one brief encounter with love in all that time. Percy said that women are different here. Emily doesn't seem "different" to me.* He squeezed her hand and she squeezed back.

Jake stood in the cool night sand of the beach. He unraveled the palm branches from around Singing Wind's offering. Emily held the light up so they could see the board. Juke pulled the last vine away and the palm branches fell to the sand.

The surfboard was carved from the blue stone.

"Look at that," Jake said. The board looked as if it were carved from glass, like some immense surfing trophy to be hung up on a wall and never touched. Jake held the board up to the blue light.

"It's beautiful," Emily said in awe.

It felt so smooth, so perfect, and then it began to glow.

At first it was a soft glow deep within the board, like a blue heart slowly beginning to come to life. There was a slow pulsing flicker of life and then gradually as if finding outgoing arteries, the whole board came to life and vibrated with breath and vitality.

Jake lifted the board high above his head. The beach glowed with light for several yards in all directions.

"It's wonderful, Jake."

"Are you sure this isn't Heaven, Emily?" Jake had the look of a man gone insane with happiness. He brought the board down to his side. They both hugged the board, feeling its warmth and each others as Jake put an arm around Emily. They were an easy target for anyone within sight of the beach.

"Do you think it will float, Jake?"

"I didn't think of that. It feels light enough." He picked the board back up. "Let's see what this baby can do. Time for some night surfing." He began to walk to the water which glistened before them in the light of the board.

"Jake?"

"Yeah?"

Emily came up and hugged him.

"Do be careful."

Jake bent down and kissed her squarely on the lips. Silhouetted on the beach they stayed embraced in the warm glow for what seemed an eternity. Emily's kiss was from a soul denied passion. He pulled away.

"I'm sorry, Jake."

"Oh, no. I understand. It's okay." He walked into the water. "I shouldn't have done that," he said, looking back at her.

She stood there, beautiful. *She could be the most beautiful woman I've ever met in my life.*

He waded deeper into the surf. The "glowboard" turned the water surrounding him into a brilliant shade of turquoise. Even the sand on the bottom was clearly visible.

He laid the board gently down into the ocean. It floated! An incoming wave washed over him, brilliantly lit as it cascaded over him. He leaped on and started paddling out, the board supporting his weight nicely.

He took one more look back at Emily. She stood with her arms at her sides and her long brown hair waved in the breeze. He paddled in the direction of the sounds of the waves breaking out at sea.

The water around him felt surprisingly warm as though heated by his glowing surfboard. Jake saw a large wave approaching, already cresting and spilling over. It threatened to collide with him. He pressed down hard and pushed the glowboard into a dive. The wave passed over him and it was then that he saw the reef. As he surfaced he swore the reef was made of the same substance as the board. Lying flat on the board, he leaned over and looked beneath the water. The reef shined in the light. It wasn't like the rocky reef back on Earth, but a smooth rolling surface. He was tempted to dive beneath the water, to touch it and feel its alluring sides.

He pulled back and sat astride the board. In the light he could make out the dim approach of another wave. The reef could wait. He quickly paddled. The mountain coming at him looked menacing and dark. There was just enough light to see its moving liquid texture. It picked him up. He gave one last shove. Standing up, he flew down the face with the light of the board showing the way.

The wave stared down at him, the black sky in the background. Jake glided up and down, challenging the wave to do something. He shot back up toward the lip, sparks of water shooting off as from a welder's torch. Then he momentarily went airborne and back down, as the foam and spit off the crest chased after him. The lip followed and enclosed him in a brilliant kaleidoscope of blue and turquoise sparkle. He flew down the glowing aqua color tube, never wanting it to end. Jake came out of the tunnel and collapsed into the sea. He swung back on the board and paddled onto the beach. Emily waded into the break and met him.

"You were wonderful. I've never seen anything so beautiful!" she cried.

"What a rush! This board is a dream!"

They walked up the beach a few paces and sat down, facing the water. Jake laid the board down beside them and stared out at the sea.

"What's wrong, Jake?" Emily noticed the smile leaving his face.

"He's out there, somewhere," Jake said solemnly.

"The Evil One?"

"Not just him. Someone else."

"Who, Jake? Who else?"

"My father."

"Your father is here? I'm sorry. You must've been young when he died."

"I was thirteen. He killed himself."

Emily grabbed his hands. "Oh, Jake."

"Shelley said that all the suicides are at a place called the Isle of Labor."

"I've heard of it. A forbidden place," replied Emily.

Jake looked at Emily sprawled out beside him. Her lovely face glowed in the soft light. He reached over and ran one of his hands through her long, soft hair.

"I'm glad I met you, Emily."

She smiled and stared at him with deep brown eyes which conveyed the same feelings and more. They came together in a tight embrace, their lips meeting halfway.

The light played with the shadows of the lovers until it began at last to fade and the board went dark again.

A long dark row of crosses burned on the beach. Menon had crucified the apostles for their failure. A lucky few had escaped, knowing that after nailing up their brothers, they too would be put to the cross. Menon cursed the Devil for his ill-preparedness. How could he do this alone? He'd searched all the islands in the vicinity. The poet said Barr has fled by boat to a nearby island. He's sent the poet to the Angel as promised, but now he wished he had him again. A little torture may have done some good. Menon went to bed, but would not sleep well this night.

He was walking through the land of dreams. Maybe here he would once again find the troubled dreams of Jake Barr. In the mist he felt a disturbance. He felt lost and confused. Something was amiss. He groped through the haze for something solid, a dream object, hopefully an object from Farr's childhood. He tripped over something. He felt around blindly. It was a bicycle. He was close. Menon continued to feel around on the cold wet surface. He felt something else. It was round and scaly. He picked it up and brought it out of the mist. It was the head of a flying demon. He gasped and dropped it. Laughter came from nearby. Menon looked nervously around.

"Who's there!"

He heard more laughter-closer now.

"I don't tolerate failure," came a familiar voice in the mist. "Am I going to have to do this myself? You know how important this is!" the voice said angrily.

Menon trembled. The Devil wasn't a forgiving soul.

"I need more! The creature has failed! The Angel's disciples are incompetent!"

"Enough!" The ground trembled under Menon's feet. "I will give you more!"

Menon hoped that was it, and that he could leave the dream realm. He felt himself jerked back into the void, hot rank breath on his neck.

"Disappoint me again and you'll be in deep shit when you get back to Hell! Understand?!"

Menon stumbled from his bed and walked, naked, onto his balcony. His eyes widened. Standing at attention before him on white sandy beaches were two hundred flying demons, all in perfectly formed rows. Two hundred clawed fists shot silently into the air and saluted him. Menon smiled.

Chapter 16

It tickled. Jake reached up and scratched his nose. He opened his eyes to find Emily hovering over him, dropping grains of sand onto his face. He quickly sat up.

"Good morning, sleepyhead," she said.

"We slept on the beach?" He wiped a large patch of sand from his face.

"Yes. I've already bathed in the sea. About time you washed up, too. Don't you think?" She gazed down the length of his body and then he realized he was naked, the wetsuit beside him. He pulled the rubbery black pile over himself and stood up, embarrassed. Emily laughed loudly-louder than she had in many years. Jake turned around, pushing a leg into the wetsuit. His sandy rear was exposed.

"Aren't you going to clean that off first?" she laughed at him. He fell over into the sand with still one leg to go. Emily walked over beside him.

"I think you need some help, dear." She pinched his rear, making him laugh.

Jake slid the wetsuit over his other leg and halfway up his body. He twisted around and grabbed at Emily's leather dress, attempting to tickle her back as she fell into the sand.

Something in the sky caught Jake's attention.

"What's wrong?" Emily asked from underneath him. She turned her head, following his gaze.

A band of twenty, small, black dots flew toward them from the sea. Jake and Emily stood and began to run back towards the woods.

"What about the board, Jake?"

"Leave it!"

They entered the woods along the path to Newt's house. Jake glanced over his shoulder. The creatures were getting closer.

"Run faster!" Jake cried, pulling Emily by the hand.

"I can't," she yelled, gasping for air.

Jake could see Newt's home just ahead now. Through the branches above them, the demons began their descent. Jake and Emily could hear the crackle of tree limbs as the monsters came crashing through. Jake saw Newt up ahead, fiddling with the hose he'd seen running from the balloon. Newt had a fire going and was sitting by it. Newt jumped up, alarmed, when he saw the sprinting pair. Singing Wind came walking out of the house.

"Get in the house!" Jake screamed. "We're being attacked."

"I knew it!" Newt yelled as he looked to the sky. He grabbed a nearby spear and ran into the house. Jake and Emily ran past Singing Wind and to the door. Jake pushed Emily inside. He turned and looked for Singing Wind. The Indian had positioned himself on one knee, his bow pulled up and firing. Two demons already lay sprawled on the grass in front of the house. The others were almost upon him.

"Singing Wind! Get in here!"

Singing Wind stood up and fired another arrow as he retreated to the door. One more demon landed with a heavy thud in the grass. Singing Wind turned and ran inside as Jake almost caught his long hair pulling the door shut behind him. Jake and Singing Wind held the door as the pounding of bodies began from outside.

Jake looked back over his shoulder and saw Newt had pulled his bed and a chair across the rear patio entrance.

Newt stood there with his spear, a dagger in the other hand. Emily stood guard, spear in hand, at the front window. Growls and hisses came from outside. Then it became quiet and the pounding on the door stopped.

"They're regrouping!" Newt cried.

"Jake," Emily said, terrified and shaking.

"It'll be okay!" Jake said back. "Think fast...what do we do?" he said to himself.

There was a sudden loud crash from the rear. Emily screamed. Jake looked back to see the demons pushing over the bed and clawing in through the archway. Newt swung the spear around wildly, its point darting in and out among the beasts. Emily ran over and stood by Jake and Singing Wind.

"Get out! I'll hold 'em off!" Newt cried.

Jake opened the front door. Singing Wind and Emily ran outside.

"Come on, Newt!" Jake screamed.

Newt turned his head back for an instant. Bloody claw marks ran across his face.

"I ain't runnin' this time, Jake! Git out of here!" Newt turned his back and continued to hold off the small horde of devil-men.

Jake walked slowly backwards and out the door. He watched as Newt bravely fought off the repeated advances of the demons. He turned and ran toward Emily and Singing Wind who were almost to the trees.

"Come! This way." Jake pointed in the direction of the balloon. He led them by following the limp hose from the house to the woods. The balloon stood firmly secured to the nearby trees.

"Okay you two, get in!" Jake yelled.

Emily pulled herself up as Jake helped her over the side of the basket.

"No," said Singing Wind.

"Don't be scared! Its okay!" cried Jake.

"Not scared. Better to make stand than hide in here like women under blanket."

"Trust me."

"Never trust white man."

Jake looked nervously around. He knew Newt was probably finished by now. "Trust this white man. No sweat."

"No sweat?" The Indian looked puzzled. Jake nodded.

Singing Wind jumped in.

Jake began cutting the support vines all around the fragile balloon as it blew drunkenly in the wind. He grabbed hold of the side of the basket and cut the last vine. The balloon shot up, leaving Jake hanging on to the side, legs dangling free in the wind. Emily screamed and grabbed at him as she and Singing Wind struggled to pull him in. A nearby tree limb flogged Jake as the balloon pulled about the forest. Jake was finally pulled over the side, landing on his head in the basket.

"On no! Jake!" Emily screamed.

Jake stood up. Emily was looking down below. Jake and Singing Wind leaned over and followed her gaze. Newt was running through the woods below in the shadow of the balloon he'd created to escape his prison. About ten of the demons were closing in and surrounding him. His weapons were gone. Newt looked skyward, raising his arms as if surrendering to his fate.

"We left him!" Emily sobbed.

"No! He told us to leave! He did it for us!"

The balloon moved higher still, passing the edge of the

forest and over the white-sand beach. Jake looked back. There was no sign of pursuit.

"We fly over great river," Singing Wind said. "Maybe Sioux on the other side."

The sea spread out below them for miles. They saw no land. Their own island was growing smaller behind them. A few fluffy clouds floated just above them in the blue sky.

"Jake!" Emily shouted. "Behind us!"

Jake looked back. Nine flying black figures were gaining on them. Jake and Emily held their spears. Singing Wind had his bow and arrows, and a dagger.

Jake looked up at the balloon. The mesh of the tied-together clothes was still holding strong. The vines were securely tied to the basket, looped up and over the top of the balloon. The creatures were growing larger behind them. Jake wondered if the balloon would survive the fight.

Singing Wind took an arrow from his quiver and steadied himself against the side of the basket.

"Feels good to hunt again," the Indian said.

"I think we're the ones being hunted," Emily said.

The creatures broke into two groups and came at the balloon from both sides. Singing Wind released an arrow and a demon went spiraling into the sea. He shot a second arrow and again a creature grasped its chest and fell seaward. The remaining devils flew about the basket, fighting for a foothold. Jake thrust his spear into the abdomen of one and pulled back as the creature fell. Emily's spear found its mark but the victim fell back, taking her spear with it. Jake spied a lone creature above, tearing at the balloon. He nudged Singing Wind who had just pulled his dagger from a wounded attacker. Singing Wind aimed an arrow. The creature fell past them, ripping a hole in the balloon as it fell to its death.

The remaining creatures came again. Jake and Singing Wind struck down two climbing over the basket.

Emily screamed behind them. The last two creatures had pulled her from the descending basket and were flying away, carrying her between them. Singing Wind pointed his bow in their direction.

"No! You might hit her or make them drop her!" Jake watched as Emily was carried away. The balloon plummeted toward the blue sea.

Chapter 17

"Land!" shouted Singing Wind, pointing wildly.

Jake looked ahead, barely seeing two, small, green blots on the horizon.

"I don't know if we'll make it there," Jake said, looking down at the approaching sea.

The wind was still blowing steadily, sending them on a course toward the island on the left. Jake could see the whitecaps on the waves below. The sea seemed to be kicking up. He could make out the beach on the island and a couple of houses. They dipped down close to the sea, the spray of a wave knocking them into the bottom of the basket.

"We'll have to swim for it!" Jake yelled.

Singing Wind nodded. The basket skipped across the waves as the balloon collapsed into the sea. The basket began to fill with water. Jake and Singing Wind jumped out into the surf and began to swim for land.

Jake crawled, exhausted, onto the beach. He looked up. The beach was deserted. He'd lost track of Singing Wind in the rough surf. Looking down the shore he sighted a pink house with a yellow roof, but saw no sign of his friend.

"Singing Wind!"

He looked out at the ocean. Maybe that Indian couldn't swim; at least not very well. He saw a dark head bobbing just offshore. Sprinting, he splashed into the water and swam toward the object. He could see matted hair floating around the dark head as he swam up. He grabbed hold of

Singing Wind under one armpit and began pulling him back to shore.

He laid him on the beach and began mouth-to-mouth on him. Singing Wind lay still.

"Come on, damn you!"

Jake tried to revive him again and then leaned back.

The Indian suddenly began to spit up water. He looked over at Jake and smiled.

"You good kisser, Jake."

"Damn you! I thought you were dead."

"Great river hard to swim."

They both stood up and looked around. They were weaponless.

"Let's head inland. If what everybody's been telling me is true, then this island should be just like the last one," Jake said.

"Where we going?" Singing Wind asked.

"To the village."

They left a dual set of footprints that disappeared into the trees.

Chapter 18

They made their way up the beach-path until they found one of the four brick roads leading to the island's center.

"So how did you get to be a surfboard shaper?" Jake asked as they entered the brick road.

"Visitor come to my island. He show me and Newt."

"So that explains Newt's longboard. Where was this visitor from? I mean when he lived on Earth," Jake said.

"He said he had lived in the land of 'Hawi'," Singing Wind answered.

"Hawaii?"

"Hawi. The Hawi tribe."

"Did he have a name?" asked Jake.

"Duke."

"Duke Kahanamoku? One of the greatest surfers ever. It must've been him!"

"He walk on water like you. He stay a few sunsets and then say he go walk on water other islands. I show him how to cut stone for arrows. He show us how to make surfboards," said Singing Wind.

Jake pulled his wetsuit up over his shoulders. He had half worn it since early morning. He pulled his arms through the rubbery sleeves. He could see buildings come into view ahead.

Once again the silence of the woods cast a foreboding atmosphere around the road.

This village appeared to be a copy of the last, with the same, Old-West facades and the names on the signs of the buildings. A woman with short brown hair sat at the café reading a book. She looked up and smiled at them as they walked into the village center. She returned to her reading, ignoring them.

"Let's go to the Pools," Jake said. He had to ask a new question. *I can ask any question I want. Any question about life. Surfing Heaven. The surfing in Heaven-what was it like?* The question had been burning in his skull.

"You ask right question, Jake," said Singing Wind, as they opened the door to the pools.

"Yes, the right question. I will, Singing Wind."

They entered the building. Once again the pools were scattered about the white, marble floor. A familiar looking figure came from the corner. The man could have passed for the twin of the caretaker at the pools of the last island. He had the gray beard to the floor, a long white robe, a wrinkled up face and hands, and the same bushy gray eyebrows.

"Would you like to see your deaths, travelers?" the old man growled.

"Let's cut right to it," Jake said. "I have a question."

"You are permitted one question," the old man replied, walking up to them in the center of the room. Singing Wind looked Jake in the eyes expectantly. Jake took a deep breath and nodded to himself.

"Emily Adams. Where have they taken her?"

"Good question," Singing Wind said.

A glazed look came over the old guy's eyes and they appeared to roll back into his head.

"She has been taken to the Isle of Labor. The abomination named Menon is keeping her captive there."

"The Isle of Labor? How do we get there?" Jake asked.

"Only one question per island," the old man said.

"Singing Wind! Ask him how we get there! You get a question too."

"How we go to Isle of Labor?" asked Singing Wind.

"By the sea," the old man said.

"But which way? How far is it? Where can we get a map?" Jake had many more questions.

"I'm sorry. No more questions. Perhaps you'd like to look into the pool to somewhere on Earth-now or in the past."

"Damn! This place is falling apart! Can't you help us?"

"You must help yourself."

"I want to see my tribe, Medicine Man," Singing Wind said.

"We really don't have time for this," said Jake.

"Come and gaze into the pool, my friend."

Singing Wind followed the old man to the fountain. Jake followed behind, looking over Singing Wind's shoulder as the images began to form. Three men and a woman, dressed shabbily, and looking dirty, sat near a dilapidated shack drinking a clear fluid from an empty mild container. They were laughing and obviously drunk. The image moved to a new group of small neglected buildings. A sign on one read, "Reservation Office." An old man sitting on the steps leading to the door appeared to be asleep.

"I have seen enough. This medicine is no good," said Singing Wind, walking away shaking his head.

"And you young man, would you like to see your home?"

"We don't have the time," said Jake. "Let's get out of here, Singing Wind."

The pair made their way to the door and exited. The woman at the café still sat reading, munching on a piece of fruit. She didn't look up as they walked outside.

"Those visions-what did they mean?" asked Singing Wind. "Those were not the proud members of my tribe."

"It must have been a mistake," Jake responded. "Let's stop here for a minute. Maybe someone on this island could be of service to us." He walked to the door of the Inn.

"I stay here and keep watch," the bronze Indian said, positioning himself outside the door.

"Suit yourself." Jake entered the Inn. He walked over to the counter and opened the Present Residents register. He read:

Name/Nationality/Occupation/Earth Years
Hermann Weber/German/Soldier/1848-1870
Tai Po/Chinese/Scientist/1918-1984
Abul Fasil/Iranian/Truckdriver/1921-1991
Catherine Walton/Irish/Wife/1855-1921
Louis Junot/French/Soldier/1780-1812
Tom Garrett/New Zealander/Tour Guide/1880-1977
Mikhail Toric/Bulgarian/Doctor/1867-1933
Jaffeny Pjormsevy/Indian/Wife/1881-1958
Amelia Earhart/American/Aviator/1898-1940
Sun Lan-chi/Chinese/Farmer/1877-1965
Alice Wright/English/Actress   /1859-1933
Arthur Thomas/American/Accountant/1929-1992
Uri Essel/Israeli/Soldier/1940-1967
Gretchen Duffy/South African/Wife/1840-1928
Alex Ochoa/Peruvian/Banker/1881-1970
Marla Torrenson/Swedish/Teacher/1866-1934
Margaret Weiss/Canadian/Writer/1911-1980
Laura Veslov/Russian/Daughter/1921-1941
Tom Bekot/Kenyan/Farmer/1931-1990

Jake leaned back. *The woman sitting outside. Can it be?* He rushed out, startling Singing Wind, who quickly stood up. The café was empty.

"The woman reading the book! Where did she go?" Jake cried.

"She leave. When you go inside Inn."

"Which way? Oh forget it. We don't have time to solve every mystery that existed back on Earth," Jake said.

"You know woman?" Singing Wind asked.

"No. I didn't know her. Which way would it be to the dock?"

"Dock?" said Singing Wind, puzzled.

"Where the boats are kept!"

"That way." Singing Wind pointed at the brick road leading out past the pools.

"There was another island next to this one. We'll take a boat there."

The sun rose straight over the village crossroads, leaving Jake and Singing Wind shadowless. They began to walk down the road out of the village and into the silent woods.

Chapter 19

"You not belong here like me, Jake," Singing Wind said as they walked down the red brick road.

"What do you mean?" Jake asked.

"I was taught since a young boy that warriors would go to a place where there are plenty of buffalo to hunt when they died. Many fish in rivers. No white men-only Indians. My people are not here."

"This is a big place. You just need to start looking for your people. There have to be a few of them here somewhere," said Jake.

"I am lost. A lost dead man."

"I don't think you're alone there, my friend," Jake replied. "You'll get to your Heaven. I have a feeling you'll find your people."

Singing Wind smiled. "You good friend, Jake."

They came to where the brick road passed over the coast path. Instead of ending there, the brick road kept going toward the sea. They walked on through more oak trees, emerging at what appeared to be a dock. A small pier jutted out into the sea. A small shack sat in front of the pier just off to one side. A grizzled man came out of the shack and stood watching them as they walked up. He was wearing a black sweater and a dirty pair of blue jeans and no shoes. The man had a wrinkled, worn face and dark, short, curly hair.

"What can I get ya?" the dockhand asked.

"We want a boat," Jake said.

"All I got left," the man said, pointing down to a couple of small canoes tied up near the shack.

"Paddles in the boats," the dockhand told him.

"You're supposed to have sailboats here," said Jake.

"They was all sunk or taken by the people of this rock. Sorry, but it's the canoes or nuthin'."

"We're going to the Isle of Labor. Do you know how to get there?" Jake asked.

The dockhand let out an insane snicker. "What the hell would you be wantin' to go to that prison for? Spent many a year toilin' away there before they gave me this job. I hope they never pull me back to that hell."

"Just tell us how to get there," Jake said.

The man laughed aloud again. "I don't know how to get there! Just know that I came from there. It's probably clear on the other side of this bloomin' place, for all I know."

"We'll take the boat. Let's go, Singing Wind." They walked down to the boat, followed by the dockhand.

Singing Wind untied the boat from a post as Jake stepped over the side and sat down. The canoe, a wooden shell with no seats, was very primitive. Two wooden paddles lay in its bottom. Jake handed one to Singing Wind, took the other and began to paddle. The dockhand stood back and watched them paddle away.

They kept the canoe parallel to the beach as they made their way around the island, searching for its neighbor.

"Remind me to grab a piece of fruit on the next island. I'm getting a little hungry," Jake said as he dipped his paddle into the sea.

The going was tough. The seas were a little rough. The small canoe struggled over hills of water that pitched around as a stiff wind blew over them. The other island came into view on the horizon. They turned the canoe in the direction of the neighboring isle and paddled onward. It appeared to be about two miles away.

"Someone leave these in boat," Singing Wind said.

Jake looked down beneath Singing Wind. There were two blue stones lying on the bottom of the canoe.

"Must be in case someone got caught out at night," Jake said.

Singing Wind took the stones and put them in his waist pouch.

The paddling was becoming very tiring. Jake was getting sore in both shoulders. Singing Wind didn't complain. Jake found himself slacking and letting the Indian power the boat alone. They were about halfway across the channel. The tree line of the new island was becoming detailed. They could make out the waving palms spread behind the white, sandy beach. Two beach houses, white with pink roofs, beckoned them closer.

Singing Wind, sitting in the port of the canoe, looked back and smiled at Jake. "You getting tired? Me working twice as hard now."

Jake resumed paddling. "Let's take her in," Jake yelled.

Singing Wind looked back past Jake.

"We are being followed. Another canoe," Singing Wind said.

Jake turned and looked back toward the last island. He couldn't see a pursuer.

"Are you sure?"

"Yep."

"Paddle faster," Jake said.

The canoe spilled over a wave into the shorebreak. They caught a small wave the last few yards as Singing Wind jumped from the canoe, landing in waist-high surf. Jake jumped into the warm waters, both of them pulling the boat onto the shore and collapsing onto the sand.

"Let's get the boat into the trees," Jake said.

They both stood and grabbed hold of the front of the canoe, dragging it over the sand and up to the trees.

They pulled the boat into the brush among the palm trees and looked back out to sea. Sure enough, another canoe appeared in the channel closing in on the island. It appeared to have a single rower. Jake and Singing Wind hid themselves, watching to see who had followed.

The pursuing canoe slid through the water and into the shorebreak. A man jumped from the boat and pulled the boat onto the shore. He paused and looked down at the beach as if puzzled by the tracks left on the sand by his query. He began to follow the trail.

"My God. It can't be," Jake cried. He stood and walked out of his hiding place to face his father.

Chapter 20

Jake walked slowly toward the man he believed to be his father. The other man had stopped and was watching his son approach. It had been twelve years, but he could still recognize his dad. He was the same tall, lanky man with high cheekbones and light brown hair. Jake walked up to his father, reeled his arm back and struck him across the chin, knocking him to the sand.

"You bastard!"

"Jake, wait," David Barr said, holding his chin. Jake's dad rose to his feet. He was dressed in a pair of beige slacks, a white T-shirt, and a pair of tennis shoes.

"You left me! Left us!" Jake cried.

"Jake, no. It doesn't have to be like this!"

Jake swung wildly, missing his father's face. "You didn't give a damn about us! How could you kill yourself and leave us all alone!" Jake was sobbing. He beat his fist into his father's chest as his father tried to hold him.

"I was sick. I still loved you," David said. Jake pushed him away.

"How can you stand there and say that? Me...Kelley, and Rick...we had to grow up without you! Didn't you want to watch us grow up? See us go out on first dates? Watch us graduate from school?" Jake sobbed uncontrollable. "See us get married?" Jake sat down in the sand. David Barr stood frozen as Singing Wind ran up.

"Him hurt you?" Singing Wind asked.

"A long time ago. Please go back to the trees, Singing Wind. I don't want you to see me like this," Jake said.

"You okay, Jake?" Singing Wind asked.

"Just go, Singing Wind!"

Singing Wind eyed Jake's dad and slowly walked back toward the trees. "You yell if you need me, Jake!" Singing Wind disappeared into the trees.

"Jake, I..."

"No. Let me finish. You abandoned me. You think I'm just going to run up to you and give you hugs and kisses now?"

"I'm sorry."

"A school kid asked me once, 'Jake, what happened to your dad?'" Jake looked deep into his father's somber brown eyes. "I said you were killed in a car accident. I was covering for you! Damn! I was too damn ashamed to tell the truth."

His father sat down beside him. "What I did was wrong. I've been punished here for it."

"Yeah, we've all been punished for it," Jake said.

"I've missed all of y..."

"Don't even start that crap! When I realized you were here I didn't even want to find you. I'm just going to finish whatever it is I'm here for and leave. I'm looking for someone, someone who cares about me and I'm going to find her."

"I can help you," David Barr said.

"Is that why you've been following us? Maybe I don't even want your help."

"I can help you find her, Jake."

"How do I know you won't just disappear again?"

"I've saved your neck once already, son. Back on your home island...the first night-you had a knife to your throat."

"That was you?"

His father nodded. They heard a disturbance back in the palm trees. Turning, they spotted Singing Wind emerging, struggling with an apostle in his grasp.

Chapter 21

Singing Wind held the man up as if he were drunk. His legs were rubbery and he leaned against the Indian for balance. The man's black hood was down around his neck, revealing the bald head and red cross. His face was all blubber and very pale.

"What's wrong with him?" Jake asked, running up.

"I hit him good. He try to surprise me. Try to get me with this." Singing Wind pulled out one of the black handled knives with a red blade.

The apostle's eyes were half rolled into his sockets and drool spilled from his mouth.

"If only Newt were here. We need information," Jake said.

"I make him talk, Jake." Singing Wind held the red blade under the apostle's throat.

The apostle recognized his own knife and suddenly looked horrified.

"Pllesshh don't cut me," he whispered before passing out in Singing Wind's arms.

"This is great. Well Dad, how do we get to the Isle of Labor?"

"We'll need to revive our bald friend here, first," David Barr said. "It looks like he's still under the influence of Menon. We could go to the spirit on this island and ask."

"You mean the old man?" Jake asked.

"Yes. He'll help us."

"Let's go then. Can you handle him, Singing Wind?"

"He plenty heavy under this blanket," Singing Wind said

as he lifted the fat apostle over his shoulder, "but I carry heavier buffalo before."

The trio walked into the woods. The afternoon sun beat down through the trees around them.

Two flying demons had been crucified in the middle of the village crossroads. The group walked up to the oak crosses and stared at the carcasses.

"Good thing no flies here," Singing Wind said.

"Looks like Menon wasn't too happy with these guys," Jake said. Jake stared closely at the grisly corpses. Wooden stakes had been driven through the creatures' hands and feet. The wings were curled over the heads at top as if the creatures had tried to shield their eyes from something.

They walked up to the café. All the fruit baskets were gone. They would have to forage for fruit in the woods. Jake led the way as they walked into the pools building. Singing Wind lay the apostle on the marble floor. The others gathered around as the old man approached from his usual corner.

"Welcome travelers," the old man bellowed. "Would you care to see your deaths on this glorious day?" The old man noticed the sprawled out apostle. "What do we have here? A sick holy man?"

"He's under the spell of evil. Our question is how to get rid of evil's influence on his soul," Jake answered.

"Very simple," said the old man. "You need a blue stone."

Singing Wind whipped out one of the stones from his waist pouch. The old man reached out a bony hand and took it.

"You had a blue stone? You really shouldn't waste your

questions, you know." The old man kneeled down beside the apostle and pressed the stone against his forehead. As the stone began to glow, the apostle shook and moaned.

"Take it away!" the apostle shouted. His body was stiff, arms at his sides. His shaking grew more convulsed. The stone seemed to grow brighter and suddenly went black. The apostle's shaking had stopped and his body went limp.

"The apostle will be renewed by tomorrow," the old man said. "Who's next?"

Jake whispered something into Singing Wind's ear.

"Emily. She okay?" the Indian asked.

The old man stood. His eyes widened and seemed to gloss over, turning white.

"The Emily you speak of is well. A prisoner, yes, but a well cared for prisoner."

"The apostle will show us the way to the Isle of Labor. Is that correct?" David asked.

"Yes. He knows the way," the old man answered, his eyes returning to normal. "No more questions. Would someone care to look at Earth?"

"Thanks, but we'll go make our camp now," Jake said.

"Camp?" said the old man. "There's no reason to camp. You can stay the night at our inn."

"Will we be safe there?" Jake asked.

"Could you please rephrase that. You're out of questions, traveler."

Jake looked at his father. "I wonder if the inn is a safe place to sleep, Dad?"

"I couldn't help but overhear the question you posed your fellow traveler," the old man said. "The inn is safe."

"Thank you," said Jake. The group made its way to the door. Jake looked back at the old man. "Are you God?"

The old man looked shocked. "Take great care about how you use that word, young man! Of course I'm not Him! And that's two questions anyway!" The old fellow shook his beard at Jake.

The group walked out into the evening sun. The crosses in the square shed long shadows, their victims' dark forms spreading across the ground. They walked over to the inn and went inside. There were six rooms down the hallway of the inn. Each of them took a room. Singing Wind laid the sleeping apostle in one of the room's beds, closing the door behind. Each room had a blue stone on the reading table next to each bed.

Singing Wind left the group to go forage for fruit in the woods.

Jake and his father stood at the counter and signed the visitors' registry.

Jake opened the current-resident register. They scanned down the list of names:

Name/Nationality/Occupation/Earth Years
Mercedes Olivas/Mexican/Singer/1892-1951
Irene Kaufman/American/Clerk/1888-1974
Ivan Pavlova/Russian/Sailor/1904-1978
Haru Tanaka/Japanese/Shop Keeper/1783-1871
Adam Krajawski/Polish/Soldier/1917-1938
Edwardo Ramos/Philippine/Fisherman/1832-1901
Tomi Chomei/Japanese/Businessman   /1938-1988
Tom Salassi/Ethiopian/Teacher/1923-1991
Sung Wei/Chinese/Carpenter/1841-1919
Elizabeth Pope/English/Stewardess/1932-1995
Sascha Zsektvay/Russian/Soldier/1924-1942
Wilbur Moore/American/Lawyer/1867-1946
Sudi Mukherjee/Indian/Wife/1781-1869
Alberto Recci/Italian/Soldier/1922-1941

Baruk Kali/Afghani/Herdsman/1887-1979
Keno Kamahana/Hawaiian/Fisherman/1844-1912
Mai Wong/Chinese/Wife/1737-1821
Red Moon/Cheyenne/Daughter/1862-1879
"Better not say anything to Singing Wind about that last entry. He'd be knocking on every door on this island."
"There are stories for all those names," David said.
Jake looked over at the thicker "Past Residents" book. He opened the dusty jacket to a page about halfway through the register. He read:
Name/Nationality/Occupation/Earth Years
Ch'eng Long/Chinese/Tool Maker/681BC-611BC
Lysus/Spartan/Wife/390BC-329BC
Thomas Abernathy/English/Farmer/1309-1350
Pirus/Roman/Artist/87-140
Eric Red Axe/Norwegian/Explorer/740-768
Suragina/Sumerian/Tabletmaker/2642BC-2601BC
Armanda Diaz /Portugese/Blacksmith/1588-1642
Bellus/Babylonian/Weaponmaker/1220BC-1182BC
Delonusix/English/Slave/44-82
Zosatep/Egyptian/Wife/3218BC-3188BC
Gantus /Mongol/Soldier/1348-1377
Militux/Celtic/Wife/387BC-332BC
Traxus /Roman/Potter /130-189
Felipe Russoi/French/Innkeeper/1322-1348
Milos/Greek/Wife/20BC-21
Dong Chang/Chinese/Shopkeeper/1661-1709
Sulavarman/Cambodian/Wife /839-892
Fayez Hamrae /Persian/Soldier/520-548
Edward Highsmith/Scottish/Candlemaker/1566-1612
Cassius/Alemanni/Wife/240-289
Tiatoxl /Mayan/Soldier/180-240
Arun Gambhirwala/Indian/Farmer/1631-1690

Pricillus/Byzantine/Wife/483-551
Marius   /Roman/Magistrate/166BC-101BC
Louis Alvarez/Spanish/Sailor/1390-1444

Jake flipped quickly through the rest of the book before closing it. "This is spooky. It's like a book of the dead," Jake said. "A book of the dead in the land of the dead."

"Hopefully they made it to a better place after their time here ran out," David added.

"When I first appeared here, I woke up in a bed. How about you?"

"Chained to a stake. I sat up in a dark, smelly place. Next, someone was handing me a sledgehammer and telling me to get to work."

"Where were you?"

"I thought I was in Hell. An apostle told me to start breaking rocks into little rocks. I just started doing it. It seemed to go on for months, years. I thought I had gone insane. Then the robed figure came back and released me. He told me I wasn't in Hell, but in a place where I had a second chance."

"Then what happened?"

"I was led through a place smelling of sweat and grime where huge wheels and turbines ran constantly like some out-of-control, industrial-age, sweat shop. Other men and women stood glued to tasks, running the machines and such. I was given the job of keeping a giant wheel oiled. Every now and then I'd get a word in with some other workers who are all suicides like myself."

"So how did you end up here?" Jake asked.

"One day two of the apostles came and told me to come with them. I was taken off the Isle of Labor to another island. They introduced me to a man named Menon. He told me if I cooperated he'd see that I'd get off labor for good."

"Cooperated with what?"

"Catching you," said David.

"Well it looks like you got me. Did you help him?"

"I landed on your island with Menon during your first night here. By then I'd realized that something was wrong. The apostles had changed and this Menon guy was up to no good. I slipped away in the confusion when they caught the poet."

"Shelley!"

"Yes. They knocked him around a little and bloodied his nose. I left when they were talking to him. There was a woman, too."

"Harriet," Jake said.

"Two of the apostles dragged her off into the woods. I followed the others to your house. That's when I saved your neck. I hit the man who was holding you."

"Thanks."

"I just kept close to you after that. I didn't know how you'd react to seeing me."

Jake was silent for a moment.

"You just can't expect me to be totally happy," said Jake. "I mean, I always wished I could talk to you. Ask you why you did it. But I also knew that I would forgive you someday too."

"I hope so," his dad answered.

Singing Wind ran in through the inn's open front door. He had several pieces of fruit in his arms. They all took a piece and bit into the fruit, quashing their hunger pains. Singing Wind took out a stone and walked over and closed the door, bringing darkness to the room. The stone in his hand began to glow, bringing back the light.

"Time to turn in, I guess," Jake said. "I'll check on our sleeping friend first."

As the others went to their room, Jake looked in on the snoozing apostle. The man was snoring uncontrollably, the fat blubber on his face shaking with each blast. Jake laughed to himself, closing the door behind him. It would be an interesting morning.

In his room, Jake found a blue stone on the reading table. He held it to bring light to the room. The walls were white with no pictures. Clean white sheets and a pillow covered the bed. He opened a small drawer on the table and found a pen and some paper.

He got out of his wetsuit and lay down in the soft bed. He reached over and took one of the pieces of paper and the pen and began to write:

The Diary of Jake Barr
My Adventures in Limbo

The pen fell to his side as Jake faded into sleep. The blue stone slowly darkened beside him.

Chapter 22

Jake found himself back in the land of dreams. The troubled dreams of hundreds of souls seemed to be penetrating him. Faces from all eras of history were floating in and out. Most just had stoic looks on their faces while others looked bewildered or terrified. Gradually, they faded into darkness and then he could see someone lying in a room with all types of tubes and machines hooked up to his body. He could see it was a hospital room. A woman stood next to the bed. The man in the bed was himself and the woman was his mother. Two others, a young man and woman, walked in. They walked up to his mother and hugged her. It was Kelley and Rick, his siblings. The scene quickly faded out and he found himself walking through a misty archway. Menon stood in the room he entered and hovered over Emily, who was lashed down to a black, rocky pyre.

"Why don't you leave? Can't you see there are people back on Earth waiting for you?" Menon cried. "When are you coming for this girl? For someone living in a high-speed, technological society, you sure are taking your sweet time getting here." Menon looked down at Emily.

"Maybe he's forgotten all about you, my sweet." Menon put a hand on one of Emily's thighs. Jake stepped closer.

"Take your damn hand off her!" Jake yelled.

Menon looked wide-eyed at him. "What's the matter, Barr? Afraid of a little...competition?" Jake lunged at him, hands outstretched. He went right through the ghoul.

"It's not that easy, surfer!" Menon laughed. He looked

back down at Emily. "She is rather lovely, I'll give you that, Barr." He leaned down, trying to kiss her.

Emily shook her head, avoiding his thin red lips. She looked over at Jake.

"Hurry, Jake! Hurry!" she pleaded.

"Hurry, Jake. Hurry, my sweet," Menon mocked. "You two make me sick. You can't stop me, Barr." He stared with dark eyes at Jake.

"You bastard! I'll kill you!" Jake yelled.

"Is that a threat, surferboy?" Menon raised his arms in the air and Jake felt his body go limp. He fell to his knees into the milky, white mists.

Jake rolled over, feeling a hand on his arm. He found himself buried in white sheets. He looked up into his father's brown sorrowful eyes.

"Wake up son. The apostle's gone."

Jake jumped out of bed and pulled the wetsuit over his naked frame.

"Dammit Dad! We need him! Where's Singing Wind!" Jake ran into the lobby, followed by his father.

Jake went out the front door. David Barr followed behind. Singing Wind was standing at the village crossroads.

"Crosses gone," Singing Wind said, turning his head back toward Jake. He was right. Someone had removed the crosses and their victims. The trio split up and began looking around the village grounds. The morning sun was not yet above the roofs of the buildings.

"Over here!" Singing Wind shouted. Jake and David ran over to him. The Indian pointed to tracks leading into the forest. Singing Wind led the way as they followed the trail into the bushes and trees.

In a small clearing they found the apostle. He was kneeling down between two dirt mounds, softly mumbling something, his eyes to the heavens. The crosses lay a few yards off to the side.

"What are you doing?" Jake asked.

The apostle jumped, startled.

"Just sendin' these lost souls off, boys," the apostle said. Jake detected a slight, southern accent.

"I think you're wasting your time on those freaks," Jake said.

"We're all God's children, son." The apostle walked over to them. "And the next thing you're gonna say is they weren't made in the good lord's image. But my sons, maybe at one time they were!" His voice rose. "Allow me to introduce myself, I'm Bobby Joe Maxwell. Now I never did feel comfortable with 'Apostle Bobby,' so you boys can just call me 'Bobby,'" he said, offering his hand to each of them. "Besides, since all Hell's broken loose 'round here, I don't think anybody'll give a damn what I'm called anymore."

"I'm Jake Barr and this is my father, David."

"How d'ya do!" Bobby said, his fat jowls curling up in a smile. "We don't get too many father and son teams 'round here."

"And that's Singing Wind."

"Hello, my son!"

Singing Wind nodded.

"Like I said, this place has gone to Hell. All on account of this feller Menon brainwashin' me and my brothers," Bobby said. "By the way, did you boys have a hand in my deprogrammin'?"

"We did. With a little help from the old man at the pools," Jake answered.

"Bless your hearts! I feel better!"

"How did you get brainwashed?" Jake asked.

"One minute I was spreadin' the word. Next, I'm called to the Angel's Isle, like many of my fellow brothers were. But it wasn't the Angel doin' the callin' from there. It was the evil or the evil makin' the Angel call us. When we were all gathered there expectin' to hear the Angel, we was all hit at once, right there. Been servin' the wrong side since then."

"Okay, but now we need to get to the Isle of Labor so we can stop this evil," Jake said. "You know the way, don't you?"

"Yes I do. But we can't leave just yet now."

"Why is that?" Jake asked.

"It can only be done at night," Bobby said.

Chapter 23

"What do you mean only at night? We're in a hurry!"

"My son, no ones ever in a hurry 'round this place," Bobby said.

"What damn difference does it make whether we leave at night or right now?" Jake pressed on, irritated. David and Singing Wind stood by, letting Jake argue his point.

"It makes all the difference," said Bobby. "At night we can travel to anywhere in this world. By day, only as far as your arms paddle or sails blow."

"There's three of us," said Jake. "We could make you take us there now."

"You can threaten me all you want to but..."

"I think he's telling the truth, Jake," David Barr said. "When we went to your island from the Labor Isle, it was at night."

"Well damn, Dad! Can't you take us there then?"

"I don't know how," David said.

"Of course he don't know how. Only apostles know the chant," said Bobby.

"Chant?" said Jake.

"It's kinda a password for the night passage," Bobby said. "If everyone knew it, we'd never catch the runaways."

"That's for sure," David agreed.

"Exactly what's on the Isle of Labor?" Jake asked.

"It's not really an island," Bobby said. "More like a damn continent! And the only place 'round here that's got mountains. Not like these flat, little islands all the same. It's like a huge factory with the roof tore off. Has a smell of sweat and burnt iron. Worse than an Alabama steel mill in July."

"Why don't the workers rebel?" Jake asked.

Bobby shrugged. "Everybody's chained up, and there's more apostles there than anywhere. The lucky apostles are out spreadin' the good word, away from that smell. But, there's been revolts-all of 'em put down. Last one led by somebody named Coburn or Corbain, somethin' like that."

The sun had begun to climb above the trees.

"So the suicides work there for two-hundred years?"

"Yep. There are furloughs, though. This ain't Hell, ya know. Do their work and they can get a soft job for awhile, like bein' a dockhand on one of these little islands."

"Seems like I'd be waiting for a soft job forever," David Barr said.

"Maybe we should go back to the village," Jake suggested. "The stench here is getting a little nauseating." Jake noticed Singing Wind had slipped away into the woods.

Jake led David and Bobby back through the woods to the village and shortly came back out into the empty square. They walked over and sat down at one of the café's tables.

"So, Bobby, how did you become an apostle?" asked Jake, after they had all become comfortable. "Were you a resident before you were an apostle?"

"Well, we're not really sposed to talk about our pasts to those we minister to, but I'll make an exception since everthin's gone to pieces. Man, I haven't felt this loose since I got here. If only a man could have a drink every once in awhile 'round this place."

"You were saying about your past," Jake prompted.

"Well, we apostles, see, we were preachers, fathers, holy

men, what have you, back on Earth. I myself was a Baptist preacher from the great state of Alabama."

"A preacher? I figured preachers would go straight to Heaven," said Jake.

"Friend, Heaven is a helluva hard place to get into on the first bat. You gotta be battin' a thousand in the morals department to get in there. Aren't too many humans, preachers included, who fit that category."

"So what tipped you up?" Jake asked.

"I had my vices, like any man. I drank the whiskey, played the cards. Had one brief affair with a church secretary that probably lowered my average a little," Bobby Joe chuckled.

"Anything else?" Jake asked.

"Hmmm...Did a few church revivals. Made the hearin', hear better, and the seein', see better, if ya know what I mean."

"So you were a chiseler, too," Jake said.

"I wouldn't go that far. We made people's faith stronger."

"So that's it?" Jake asked.

"Well, I led the prayer at a KKK meetin' once, but I wasn't no member. Said they needed a preacher to lead the prayer at a civic meetin'. It was civic alright. The mayor, chief of police, and even the high school principle was all there. That was the night they lynched poor Tommy Winchester." Bobby looked down at his belly.

"You stood by while a man was lynched?" Jake cried.

"By God, if I had said anythin' they'd a lynched me too! That was 1965, the year I died," said Bobby Joe.

"How did that happen?" David asked.

"I was on my way home from a revival. A train beat me

through a railroad crossin'. I just hope the gal with me made it."

"Your wife?" Jake asked.

"Nope. It was that secretary. Just givin' her a ride home, mind ya."

"You were a mess, Bobby," said Jake.

"Let him without sin throw the first stone."

"So how did you get away from Menon?" David jumped in.

"An awful scene. He began to crucify many brothers. I was made to help with the first few crucifixions. He blamed us for not catchin' Jake. When I realized that I would be killed too, I snuck off. They were crucified on the beach on the other side of this island, just like those two poor devils you saw here."

"And you were going to use that knife against us?" asked Jake.

"I was still under the evil's influence," Bobby said. "By the way, what happened to that knife?"

"Singing Wind kept it. He's probably making spears with it, or arrowheads," said Jake.

"He must be careful with that knife! It's no ordinary knife!" Bobby shouted as though back at a revival.

"What's so special about it?" Jake questioned him.

"Those black blades were forged in Hell. If you're cut by one, there'll be no reawakenin' here! You'll be on a fast train to see the Devil!" cried Bobby Joe.

Jake almost had an urge to shout "Amen!"

"So that's why the apostle said I had doomed him to Hell," said Jake.

"You killed a brother?" asked Bobby, the fat on his forehead curling up.

"He wasn't normal, and there were two of them. It was self-defense."

"Did you kill him, too?"

"He ran away," said Jake.

"Awful to kill here, just awful," moaned Bobby.

"The boy said it was self-defense," said David.

Suddenly a man ran shouting into the square. "Father! Father!" He stopped in front of Bobby Joe and dropped to his knees. The man had short black hair and wide, dark, expressive eyes.

"What is it my son?" Bobby said, falling back into his apostle character.

"My name is Alberto Recci, and I have sinned," the man said, kissing the apostles feet. He was dressed only in a pair of dirty white shorts, his chest hairy and tan. There was a bloody scratch across one of his cheeks.

"Sit up, Alberto my son, and tell me the nature of your sin."

The man seemed to regain some composure. "I touch a woman, father. She no alike it. Say she's agonna tell on me. Her name, father is Irene Kaufman. I thought she like me, father."

"Why did you think that, my son?"

"Cause she tell me she like me! And she holda my hand. So, I kiss her. And then she scream like I'a hit her. Say she's a married for sixty years ona Earth, and still married."

"I see," said Bobby, loving the gossip.

Jake and David looked at one another and silently laughed.

"I tell her, death do them apart. Not married anymore. Am I right, Father?"

"Now son, that's up to the parties involved."

"I know Father. I tell her, 'Why you not with a you' husband?' The fathers can afind him for you if he's ahere. She say she not gonna hunt for him. He gotta make'a the first move. I say how longa you been here, Irene? Twenty-one years, she tell me."

A woman walked into the square. She was wearing a long white robe that flowed behind her on the ground. She ran quickly over toward Alberto, who got behind Bobby Joe.

"You jerk!" she yelled. The woman had long, dark hair and a slender face with large, brown eyes.

"Thatsa the woman, Father. Keep her away from me!"

Jake and David backed up a few paces. The woman tried to get around Bobby, while Alberto kept using him as a human shield.

"He tried to have his way with me, a Christian woman." She reached around Bobby, pawing at Alberto.

"Now you two better settle down if we're gonna solve this," Bobby advised. "Irene? Did Alberto make an unwanted pass at you?"

"It was more than a pass! We were sitting on the beach talking when all of a sudden he rolls over on top of me!"

"You like me. You wanted me," Alberto said. "I can tell those things in a woman."

"You trash!" yelled Irene. "I'm a Christian woman and still married!" She reached out, grabbing for him and pushing Bobby aside. Alberto escaped and she began to chase him around the square.

"I tol' you she want me! Look how she'sa chasing me!"

Irene screamed as she ran behind him.

"You just wait 'til my husband finds me! He'll take care of you!" Alberto ran down one of the brick roads and out of the village, Irene giving chase behind.

Bobby Joe had stood up during the chase and walked over to where Jake and David stood watching the theatrics.

"I'd better go minister to them." Bobby followed the path of the mad duo. "I'll be back at sunset."

"Meet us here!" Jake yelled. Bobby only waved back as he disappeared down the red brick road.

"People come and go quickly around here," Jake said.

Chapter 24

Jake and David Barr stood alone in the square on an island somewhere in Limbo with a day to kill before them. The sun was climbing across a perfect blue sky.

"Let's go back to the pools," Jake said.

"We've already asked our questions here," his father said.

"I know. I want to look at something."

Jake began walking toward the pools building, his dad behind him. They entered and walked up to one of the fountains. The water glistened in the torch light. They were soon joined by the old man.

"Welcome back, travelers. How can I be of service?" the old fellow said, a little groggy, as if he'd just awakened from a nap.

"I want to look at the past. In there," Jake said, pointing at the glimmering water.

"Very well. Your death?"

"No. You really do have a death hang-up, don't you?" Jake asked. "Show me Santa Monica, California. It was about two o'clock in the afternoon. The day before my father's death." Jake looked over at his dad.

"Jake, you don't have to…"

"Yes, I do."

"Very well young man. That would be the Earth year of 1982. Where shall we look?" asked the old man.

"Just show me where I was," Jake answered.

The water in the pool began to cloud up and darken. A swirling murky whirlpool soon turned into a calm picture of the inside of a car. Jake and his younger sister, Kelley, were being driven by Jake's dad. It was his old Fiat sports car.

"Show me fifteen minutes ahead of this," Jake said.

The old man nodded. David Barr looked confused, unsure of his son's intentions.

The car was now parked in front of a house. The houses were tightly packed together in typical, middle-class Californian style of those neighborhoods that sprung up in the seventies. David Barr stood at the front door, talking to a woman with long red hair. They appeared to be arguing. Jake and Kelley sat bored in the Fiat out front. After a couple of minutes, David walked quickly across the front lawn and got back in the car with his son and daughter. The red sports car quickly sped away.

"That's enough," Jake exhaled. "Who was that woman, Dad?"

"Jake, that was a friend I…"

"You thought we were too young and stupid then to know. I was thirteen years old. I knew, Dad. Who was she?"

"Give me a break, Jake."

"Tell me who she was."

"What else may I assist you gentlemen with?" the old man asked.

"Let's go back outside." Jake walked to the door and exited, his father pulling the door shut behind. "Dammit. It's been thirteen years. I want to know what happened. You were having an affair right?"

"Yes," his father answered.

"Is that why you ended your life? Because both of the relationships were ending?" Jake wiped the sweat from his eyes, or were they tears?

"Part of it. I was sick. I must have been," his father offered.

Jake looked down and shook his head. "I've had all these questions built up inside me for so long."

"I'm sorry," said his father.

"C'mon. I need to find a pond to wash off in," said Jake. They walked out of the square and into some surrounding oak trees.

"You know, there was something else," Jake said.

"What?" David asked, expecting the worst.

"I know you're not going to remember this, though."

"Try me," his father said.

"You were driving. You had me and Rick in the car with you. I must have been about five—Rick about seven."

"Okay."

"You said something that I never forgot," Jake said.

"What was that?"

"Never get married."

"I see. Your mother and I must've had a fight."

"I always thought, 'How could a father say something like that to his own kids?' Did you mean you wished you had never married Mom and that we had never existed?"

"Of course not. It was a figure of speech..."

"A pretty damn powerful figure of speech," said Jake. "I admit, it didn't mean much to me at the time, but over the years it sunk in more and more. I guess you'll be happy to hear that I've followed your advice."

"I just wanted all you kids to be happy."

"Yeah, Dad."

They walked on through the silent forest. They passed a forest home and decided to keep on walking, leaving the resident undisturbed if he were there.

"So you're blaming me for your not getting married?" David asked.

"Well, after you find your father dead by his own hand, it gets a little hard to trust or get close to anyone for a long time."

"I didn't mean for that to happen. I thought you were with your mother."

"No, if you had remembered, I had spent the night with Mark Holder down the street."

They walked out from among the trees to the edge of a blue pond. Jake sat down on the bank, his legs dangling in the water. He reached down and splashed water into his face. His father kneeled on the grass beside him.

"You turned out to be a pretty good surfer, son."

Jake turned his head quickly. "How do you know that? I really didn't get going 'til after you were gone."

"There are pools on the Isle of Labor. I wanted to see what you were doing. The apostles figure it's punishment if we can see what we missed," said David.

"Did you watch me find your body?"

"Many times."

Jake cupped both hands together and splashed his face again. The oak trees surrounding the pond bore silent witness to the father and son meeting in eternity.

Jake stood up and stared down into the water.

"I think I'm gonna wake up in a hospital," said Jake. "I'll start blabbering about you and this place. They'll think I'm nuts!"

David stared into his son's eyes. "If that's where it goes then you don't have to tell anyone. If this helps you get it off your chest then something good will come from it."

"But what about Rick and Kelley? Mom?"

"I saw you again," David said. "Hopefully I'll see them again, but under better circumstances."

"Do you still love Mom? She's remarried now."

"I'll always love her. And I hope her new husband is good to her," answered David.

They began walking back in the direction of the village. The noon sun beat down from above. A slight breeze rustled the oak and palm branches above them.

"I'm sorry I hit you. I just couldn't help myself," said Jake.

"It's okay. I can't blame you."

They could see the buildings of the village ahead. The square was empty.

"Let's go back to the pools. I want to show you something," said David.

Chapter 25

"Show me Pickett's Charge, Battle of Gettysburg, 1863," David Barr said to the old man.

"Very well," said the old fellow.

The pool cleared to show a green, summer, Pennsylvania field. A massive amount of gray-clad men were marching into a sea of exploding cannon fire. They began to drop randomly. The men marched faster. Musket fire began to open up, further depleting their ranks. Now Jake could see a long blue line, the goal of the now running, gray hoard. The musket fire grew more intense and the gray fell by the thousands. They swarmed up to the blue line, a few spilling across, being killed or captured. The rest retreated back across the field of death. The vision in the pool grew dim and vanished and the pool returned to its crystal clear water.

"You try it son," said David. "We can time-travel right here. The sound is just turned down."

Jake thought about it. Anywhere in history? "Show me some Christians being thrown to the lions."

"That's gruesome, Jake!" said his father.

"That would be ancient Rome, no doubt," said the old man. "That could fall within several years. I will select one randomly."

The pool cleared once again and the tall, white walls of the Colosseum appeared, surrounding thousands of brightly-clad, bloodthirsty Romans sitting on their marble tiers. A large awning hung overhead, protecting them from the sun. The vision in the pool closed in on the large, dirt floor. A small group of about twenty men and women were huddled together praying. Suddenly, two red flags were waved at one end of a surrounding wall. A gate opened slowly and three lionesses and a lion darted out. The Romans in the stands stood up and waved madly. The ribs on the beasts could be clearly seen. The Christians on the floor didn't move as the beasts saw them and approached.

"That's enough!" Jake shouted, raising his hands.

The vision quickly faded.

"There must be something in history we could look at that doesn't have to do with blood," said David. "Happy historical events, hmmm...VJ Day. First man on the moon."

"Our house in Iowa," Jake said.

"What?" said his father.

"The house in Iowa we lived in. Before we moved to California. The last time we were happy as a family."

"What city, what year?" said the old man.

"Indianola. 1980."

"Behold," said the old man.

A small white, wooden home with black shutters and a white picket fence across the front came into focus. A sidewalk led from the front door to a red gate in the fence, slicing in two a neatly-trimmed front lawn. Red flower boxes with yellow tulips hung from the windows. A tire swing hung from a single tree in the yard.

"Looks like no one's home," said David.

"It looks sad. Like it knew we were about to move," Jake said. "Houses love kids. It's when they grow old and leave that the paint starts to fade."

A green station wagon pulled in front of the house. Jake shivered at the sight of the car. His dad got out of the driver's side, his mother the passenger side. The rear of the wagon popped open and young Jake and his brother and sister plopped out, running in through the gate. A command from his father sent the kids back for a bag of groceries apiece. The family disappeared into the house.

"One big happy family," David said.

"I hate that car," said Jake.

"Hate or hated?" his father said.

"I still hate it. I could never get into another station wagon after what happened," Jake said.

The vision in the pool began to blur.

"Let's get out of here," said Jake.

Jake and David walked back over to the café and sat down. A woman walked quickly from around the corner of the café and approached them.

"Is there an apostle around?" the woman said, sitting down at their table. She looked rather distressed. She had long, blonde hair and blue eyes, and was wearing a floral print dress.

"Uh, no. Not lately," said Jake.

"My name is Elizabeth Pope and I must find my husband. He must be dead by now! My Lord, he's got to be in his nineties by now!"

Jake and David introduced themselves.

"You see, Henry remarried in later years to a much younger woman. The woman was after his money, I just know it. He would want to be with *me* in eternity, not her. Why would you want to spend eternity with someone who's just after your money?"

The two men shrugged.

"When he gets here he'll realize who really loved him," the woman said, rising to her feet. "I must find an apostle!

Henry will be here soon! I just know it!" She began to walk quickly across the square, onto one of the red, brick roads. "I just know it!" She disappeared into the woods.

"Poor Henry," said David.

"Possessive, even beyond the grave," said Jake. "Dad, how come you're not young again like other people around here? You still look like you did last I remember. You were in your late thirties. Right?"

"The suicides stay at the same age when they died. Most are young anyway, but there are some old-timers, too."

"The dockhand did look a little old, now that I think about it. What about children?" asked Jake.

"As far as I know there are none here. No one under sixteen appears here. That's what I overheard."

"Where do they go?" asked Jake.

"I don't know. Maybe Heaven or maybe reincarnated for another shot at life on Earth." An apostle said they have the eternal sleep until their parents or parent arrives.

"Who doesn't make it here? Jake asked.

"I never heard of any murderers, rapists, or child molesters being here. Or any real, hard-core criminals, for that matter," David said.

"So they go straight to Hell then?" asked Jake.

"I don't know. It would be nice to think that. Maybe they go somewhere like this, only worse but not quite Hell- a second chance. Not that they deserve it," said David.

"So you believe this really is the religious master plan we were all supposed to be so well prepared for?" Jake asked.

"Until anyone proves otherwise, I believe it," said David. "You still have doubts, after all you've seen?"

"It's just not what we were taught."

"But that matters little here. You were taught to be good, at least as good as you could be. Good enough to get here," said David.

Shadows fell on them from overhead. Jake looked up and saw several flying creatures high in the sky. He stood up quickly.

"C'mon Dad, we've got to take cover!"

David stood and followed Jake into the woods.

Chapter 26

Jake and David hid themselves in bushes near the square. A tall oak tree towered above them. Six of the creatures glided in and landed in the crossroads. The demons spread out and began to look around. They ran in a hunched, comical gallop, their wings folded in behind them. One creature pulled and tugged at the Inn door, but it wouldn't budge.

"The old man was right about the inn. He can't get in," whispered Jake to his father.

Two other creatures pulled at the door to the pools. The door wouldn't open. One got into the clothes building, while another was in Books. The last snooped around the café, upturning chairs and tables and examining the ground. It then looked up in the direction of the hidden pair. Jake was certain they'd been found out.

"Maybe we should run for it. We have no weapons," Jake whispered.

The creature began to hop towards them.

"Wait," David said quietly, gesturing towards the sky.

Another creature was flying over the square. It waved frantically at the six on the ground. A single arrow stuck from one of its legs. It pointed for the others to follow. A low growl came from its mouth. The creatures in "Books" and "Clothes" came rushing out, joining their companions.

The creature walking towards Jake and David stopped and looked up at its wounded ally. The other five on the ground were now taking flight, swarming up and around the wounded one. The creature was now only a few feet away from Jake's position, its black eyes seeming to stare right at him. Suddenly it flapped its great, gray wings and turned back towards the square, ran a few steps, and began to ascend into the blue sky. The entire group disappeared over the treeline.

"Sounds like Singing Wind has reinvented the bow," said Jake. "I hope he is okay." Several more creatures flew overhead in the direction the earlier group had flown.

"I had half a mind to let them catch me. I'm in a hurry to find Emily. Maybe they would've taken me to her."

"Or ripped you to pieces," David said.

"It's still only early afternoon. I can't handle this waiting," Jake said, as he kicked a nearby bush. His foot connected with something hard, and he cussed at the pain.

Jake crawled over to the hard object hidden in the bushes. His dad stared skyward, watching for the enemy. Jake pushed the brush apart. There was an object sticking out of the ground. It was a metallic pipe which looked like a periscope above water, slightly curved protruding about a foot above the ground.

Chapter 27

"What is it Dad?"

"I've never seen anything like that around here," David answered.

The gray pipe was firmly planted in the ground. Jake put his ear to the end which opened. He could hear a low, humming noise coming from somewhere below. "Listen. Do you hear it?" he asked.

"Sounds like some kind of machine."

"There must be an opening around here-a way to get down there," said Jake. They crawled around in the general vicinity of the pipe, but found nothing.

"Maybe all's not what it appears here," said Jake.

Something rustled in the bushes nearby. Jake and David became still. Whatever it was came closer, crawling through the bush toward the square. Jake sneaked over and pounced. He pulled up a shaking Bobby Joe Maxwell.

"Don't hurt me! It's just me," Bobby whispered urgently. "Whew! I thought you was one of them flyers."

"Yeah, you're lucky I didn't jump on your skull," Jake said. "We've got something to show you. C'mon."

He led Bobby over to where David was hidden, and pushed the bushes back to reveal the pipe.

"Ahh-ha," said Bobby.

"Don't ahh-ha us. What is it?" Jake asked.

"Can't tell ya."

"Look. Either you tell us or you're gonna be demon bait," Jake threatened.

"Look son, you'll be back here in seventy or so years.

You don't really wanna go spoil all the mystery of this place in just a few short days, now do ya?" Bobby pleaded.

"I want to know, too," David said.

"But you see, boys, we apostles are sworn to secrecy on some things. The way-stations are one of them."

"Way-station. What's that?" Jake asked.

"I can't tell ya."

"Demon bait, Dad?"

"Demon bait," agreed David.

"Okay," Bobby resigned. "It's underneath us right now. The way-stations are for the apostles."

"We want to go down there," said Jake.

"Now Jacob! You're pushin' it! I could lose my position!"

"It's Jake. I don't care. How do we get in?"

The shadows of several more flying demons passed over the square. Bobby looked up and shivered. "Okay, follow me!"

Bobby kneeled over and sneaked slowly through the woods toward the back of the "Books" building. He walked up to the rear wall and pressed in a small section, pulling a panel sideways and revealing a narrow passageway with stairs leading downward. He pulled a blue stone out and motioned for Jake and David to enter. Bobby pulled the panel closed behind them as they walked down the gray steps, the stone lighting the way. It was damp, smelling like a wet basement. They reached the bottom of the stairs and were now walking down a long, narrow passage. Jake and David had to stoop down as they walked to avoid hitting their heads. They came to an archway which opened into a large, cold room. Something was humming inside.

"Ahhh, the ante-chamber," Bobby said in his best Bela Lugosi voice.

The light revealed a large room with a bed, couch, and file cabinets. The humming was emitted by two, metallic crates in a corner.

Jake walked over to the crates. "What's this?" Jake asked.

"Just the electric generator and air conditioner," Bobby said. "It does get a bit warm, with all the travel we do and all."

"You have electricity down here?" Jake cried. "I suppose you have a television and VCR too. Maybe a cold brew in the fridge?"

"No, nothin' like that. Maybe some islands have more," Bobby said, sitting down on the king-size bed.

"The poor slobs on the surface have nothing while you apostles are staying in executive suites," Jake said.

"Now I wouldn't go so far as to say that. It was no picnic bein' a preacher or rabbi, or whatever back on Earth. I guess we earned a few perks," said Bobby.

"I think you were enjoying a few perks on Earth," said Jake.

"Over here, Jake," David said, who was looking through the file cabinets. "There are files here on everyone on this island, and a photo too." Jake walked over to the file cabinets. There was Alberto Recci's file, with a photo of Alberto sitting at the café. Apparently, he didn't know his photo had been taken.

"You have cameras here?" Jake asked.

"I can't deny that one. You got the proof," said Bobby.

"This man didn't know he was being photographed. Did he?" asked Jake, holding the photo up.

"Well, we don't want anybody getting' the wrong idea. It's just our way of keepin' track of everybody. The next brother that comes along will easily know how each resident is doin' on their road to salvation."

There were notes scribbled in each person's file. A confession here, a plea for forgiveness there, and so on. There was also a brief background sketch of each person's life on Earth. The file cabinet had a single drawer. The next one had six drawers and read, "PAST RESIDENTS". David kept looking over the current residents' files. Jake opened the top drawer of the past residents' file cabinet. He pulled a file out randomly.

"Lasodius. Greek. 522BC-471BC," Jake read. He opened the file and stared down at a photo of a short, muscular man. Once again the photographer had caught the subject sitting at the café.

"Hmmm, a man from Ancient Greece," said Jake. David looked over his shoulder and stared. The file slipped out of Jake's hand and scattered to the stone floor.

Jake noticed what looked like a door near the bed where Bobby had been sitting. While Bobby was busy picking up the file, Jake walked over and pushed on the door. It opened. He stepped inside.

"Oh my God! I don't believe it!" Jake cried.

Chapter 28

"Get out of there!" Bobby yelled, running into the room.

Jake stood looking at a wall of video screens. On each screen was either the den or bedroom of each house on the island. There were five rows across, four in each row. Two buttons were under each screen. Two screens off to the side gave two separate shots of the village square. A cozy-looking easy chair faced the screens.

"This is insane," Jake said. "What kind of a place is this?" Jake moved closer to the screens.

"Incredible," said David, pushing aside Bobby.

"You mustn't be in here! You've seen enough already!" Bobby pleaded.

Jake studied the screens. On one, a resident sat calmly at home reading a book. On another, a woman lay in bed, staring blankly at the ceiling. A name and number was posted under each screen. On one screen labeled "Kaufman," Jake could see Alberto, trying his best to make up with the irate woman who'd chased him around the square earlier.

"This is sick," Jake said. "Why?" Jake looked at Bobby.

"We have to monitor their progress. Can't you see? How can we monitor their progress if we can't see them all the time?" Bobby asked.

"I think there's a higher power that's supposed to do that," said Jake.

"Jake," said David, pointing at the screen in the bottom corner.

It was Singing Wind. He was sitting down next to an

open window, a new bow at his side. He was perspiring heavily, his chest rising and falling rapidly. A woman with long, dark hair, also armed with a bow, faced the opposite direction. Singing Wind stood and let an arrow fly out the window.

"They're trapped!" said Jake.

"And it looks like he found Red Moon after all," said David.

"These buttons! What do they do?" Jake shouted.

"Nothing!" Bobby pleaded.

Jake pressed the left button under the screen showing the trapped pair. The screen went dark. He quickly pressed it again. The picture reappeared. He tried the right button. He could now hear Singing Wind's rapid breathing. Singing Wind stood and rapidly fired off two more arrows. He shouted to the girl, "Come!" They disappeared out the window. Jake kept watching.

Seconds later, three flying demons galloped clumsily across the den floor and out the window, tracking the duo. Jake reached up and hit the left button again, darkening the screen.

"We've got to help him!" cried Jake, who took a few steps towards the door.

"I think we should stay put," said Bobby. "It will be getting' dark soon so he's probably headin' this way."

"But he needs our help," said Jake.

"Looked to me like Singing Wind's the type that can take care of himself," said David. "I agree with Bobby. Let's wait here."

"Look on the city screen," said Bobby. A large group of demons had landed in the square-there must have been at least fifty of them. They began searching the area.

"What if they stay there all night," said Jake.

"I will say a prayer for them not to," said Bobby.

"A lot of good that'll do," said Jake. He looked up at the screens. The woman who had been staring up at the ceiling was now being rousted from bed by two demons who looked under the bed as she jumped into a corner, melting into the floor and crying hysterically. On another screen, Alberto Recci and Irene Kaufman ran out onto the balcony of Irene's beach house as a horde of creatures ransacked the home.

"Oh my-this is gettin' bad," said Bobby, wiping his brow. The creatures in the square began to take flight into the sky, except for four who stood still at the crossroads, facing one another. The four creatures had become like statues, guarding the village.

"Looks like we may have a little problem," said David.

"If we can get quietly out the back without bein' noticed, then we can slip into the woods and get away," said Bobby.

"Don't forget Singing Wind," said Jake.

"We won't have time to look for him if he doesn't show up, you realize," Bobby said.

"He'll show," said Jake. "I can't believe you guys. You call yourselves brothers, but big brother is more like it. Couldn't you just leave it up to these people to be good or bad here on their own. Is all this really necessary? Isn't it up to God to know who's sinned or not?"

"But how can we help them if we don't know the progress their makin' towards salvation?" pleaded Bobby.

"This is obscene!" said Jake. "Do you sit there and watch if a man and woman decide to make love or if a person decides to masturbate?"

"Hopefully it won't come to that!" said Bobby urgently.

"Well in case you didn't notice, people are still in human form here, not some gaseous spirits. And they're still acting human," said Jake.

"I think you underestimate the human ability to achieve saintliness," said Bobby.

"I think you overestimate it," said David.

"Oh no. That's the reason for all this. We know that sin will occur. But if we catch it and nip it in the bud, then maybe there's hope for the sinners to cleanse themselves in the ponds of repentance," preached Bobby.

"You mean the ponds on these islands?" asked Jake.

"Yes," answered Bobby.

"I think this whole place is insane," said Jake. "It's ruled by an Angel of Madness."

"Mad? A little eccentric maybe, but she's not mad," said Bobby.

"She?" said Jake.

Chapter 29

"Yes, a woman. Ozimadus, the Angel. Our leader," said Bobby. He bowed his head as he spoke here name.

"What does she look like?" asked Jake.

"The perfect woman. Oh such beauty! She would put a Helen of Troy to shame! That is why no one may gaze upon her."

"Why not?" Jake asked.

"She's a real looker. A fellow who looks at her will go looney. Sometimes she walks the Earth driving guys nuts just from a whiff of her perfume," Bobby continued.

"So much for just eccentric," said David.

"Why doesn't she just stop Menon?" asked Jake.

"She's under his thumb. He's nuts and I'm afraid she's in love with him."

"What?" Jake said.

"She is lonely. No man was able to approach her here and on Earth she was only a phantom. Menon has given her hope."

"Hope for what?" Jake asked.

"Why, love of course," answered Bobby. "She's like a farmer's daughter. She'll run away with the first one who gets past her daddy."

"Who's her daddy here?" asked Jake.

"Whoever he is, his back has been turned lately," said Bobby. There was little activity on the screens now. The frightened woman still sat in a fetal position curled up in the corner even though the creatures were gone.

"Perhaps we should go back into the master room," said Bobby. "You've seen all there is to see in here."

"I'll stay and watch the square," David said, collapsing into the easy chair. "In case Singing Wind comes back early."

"Have it your way," replied Bobby.

Jake and Bobby walked back out into the next room. Bobby fell down on the bed.

"I could catch up on a nap about now," the apostle said.

Jake walked back over to the file cabinets. The Greek's file was laid upon an open drawer. He put it away, walked over to the sofa and sat down. It was soft and cool.

"So at the end of two-hundred years, do you apostles pull the files and decide who's been naughty and who's been nice? Maybe write an 'x' in a box that says, 'to hell,' or wherever," Jake said.

"Nothin' of the sort," Bobby said. "We're just like some glorified case workers. We don't make the final judgment. It's like you said-up to a higher power."

"After seeing your voyeur center, I can't really trust what you say," said Jake.

"You are quite the doubtin' Thomas, Jake," said Bobby, turning over on his side, away from Jake.

Jake sank into the sofa. If felt like a big soft marshmallow.

"I just don't like surprises," said Jake.

The blue stone next to Bobby grew dim and finally went dark, throwing the room into complete night.

Jake was riding his bicycle. This time he was grown, his legs clumsily pedaling in uneven circles. He was in his wetsuit. He coasted the bike into his yard and fell off. The bike careened into the side of the house. He looked up to see Newt Worley and Singing Wind marching slowly and blankly towards him from around the house. They carried black bladed daggers, outstretched in his direction. Jake ran over to the side gate at the other corner of the house. From nearby, several dogs were howling as if in great pain. His pursuers were gaining on him. "Newt! Singing Wind! Wake up! It's me, Jake!" he shouted at them.

They didn't respond, but only walked on, trampling his mother's tulips in their blind pursuit. Jake heard a car idling nearby. He swung the gate open and entered the back yard. There were pale, naked bodies strewn like sardines across the lawn, surrounding the green station wagon which sat running in the middle. He recognized the bodies as some of the people he'd met in Limbo. He carefully stepped over Alberto's carcass. A putrid stench filled his nostrils. He tripped and fell upon Elizabeth Pope's naked body. He stared into her lifeless eyes. Perhaps they were looking for Henry? Jake quickly rose to his feet.

The gate swung open behind him. Newt and Singing Wind came walking slowly through, their eyes fixed upon him. Jake stumbled forward over the body of Irene Kaufman. A broken smile was fixed upon her lips and her open eyes stared skyward. Jake was near the car now. Its windows were misty, and the red rag waved at him from the exhaust. Menon stepped around the front of the car from where he'd been hiding. Jake froze.

"So glad you could come to our little show, Jake," Menon leered as he walked over to the driver's door. Jake felt cold steel press against his throat as Newt embraced him from behind, Singing Wind at his side. They pushed him forward toward the car. Menon opened the door. To his horror, Jake watched as his father's limp body fell out onto the grass.

"You bastard!" Jake yelled.

"Who me? Or him?" Menon said, shaking his head. Jake

was pushed on through the door. He coughed as the fumes rolled out.

"Like father, like son. Huh, Jake?" Menon laughed. "I warned you to leave!"

Jake struggled in the grip of his entranced friends. He was pushed into the driver's seat...

⤴

Jake came out of his dream and looked up at Bobby Joe, who was shaking him. He pushed back, only halfway out of the dream.

"Wake up! Damn ya!" Bobby shouted.

Jake sat up and shook his head.

"Some nightmare you were havin' there, son. Looks like we all took a little nap."

"Is it sunset yet?" Jake asked.

"I don't know. Let's go look at the screen." They walked into the other room, Bobby leading the way with the light from the stone. David sat snoozing in the easy chair. Bobby walked over and roused him, as Jake looked at the screens. They were all black.

"Dad must have turned them all off." It stayed black. Bobby and David walked up next to him.

"They're not working," Jake said, quickly pushing several of the buttons.

"They still work," said Bobby. "Sunset has come and gone!"

Chapter 30

David watched the video screen as a blue stone bounced hard in the middle of the square, its light showing the bodies of three dead demons with multiple arrows stuck in their scaly bodies. Bobby Joe stuck his head through the door.

"Well?" the apostle asked.

"Three dead and one missing. That's it," said David. There was a movement from the trees. "Wait! There's something else!" David watched as Singing Wind and Red Moon came from the trees, their bows at the ready. The pair walked stealthily over to the stone, crouching near their victims and waiting.

"It's them! Tell Jake!" David shouted. Bobby's head disappeared. David watched the screen as his son ran out into the square, embracing Singing Wind and meeting Red Moon. Bobby Joe's head reappeared.

"Let's go, David! Time to leave!"

The group made their way from the village and into the woods. Bobby steered them toward the dock.

The woods were filled with the sound of low snarls, howls, and the hissing of the demons. Jake's group moved cautiously, trying to stay undiscovered. Bobby held a blue stone up for light.

"Cover that up," Jake whispered.

"We have to see where we're going!" Bobby said. There were movements and noises all around them. The stone reflected glowing, red eyes.

"Why don't they attack?" Jake asked.

"Something's got them spooked," said David. "Maybe they're afraid of Singing Wind and Red Moon." Singing Wind paused occasionally to let fly an arrow in the direction of the eyes or a noise, sometimes emitting a howl of pain.

"Maybe it's the stone," said David.

"What?" Jake and Bobby said in unison.

"Remember the old man said it drove the evil from Bobby? He said there's good inside it. Maybe that's what the creatures fear."

Bobby held the glowing stone up higher. The growls and hoots continued, but still there was no rush of the hoard around them from the forest.

"Anyone else have one?" Bobby asked.

"Yes," said Singing Wind. He pulled out a stone from his waist pouch for each member of the party. "Red Moon and me collect for us all. These too!" He reached down and pulled out blue-bladed daggers for everyone.

The group continued forward. Each member held a stone high in the air, filling the forest with a brilliant glow which drove the creatures farther away.

"The dock should be just ahead," Bobby said.

The dock was deserted. Jake ran ahead, spotting four canoes on the right side of the pier. He looked inside the small shack where the dock-hand normally sat. It was empty. The others quietly began boarding two of the canoes. Singing Wind and Red Moon climbed into one. Jake joined Bobby and David in another, sitting down in the stern.

The calm sea around them lit up as they paddled away from the dock. There was no pursuit from the forest behind.

"Now where?" said Jake.

"Keep rowin'," Bobby answered. "Out to sea." The two boats quietly plowed through the water, occasionally climbing over small, smooth, ocean ripples and waves. The long dark outline of the island was left behind.

Bobby leaned over the side of the boat as Jake and David paddled. He held his blue stone under the water and lowered his head to the water's surface, as if searching for something.

"Here! Stop here!" Bobby cried.

"Why here?" asked Jake, as the canoes came to a halt.

"The reef. We are above the reef," said Bobby. "Bring the canoes together." Singing Wind and Red Moon paddled their canoe up against the side of the other.

"Now everyone lay down in their canoe, please," Bobby ordered.

"Why? What are you doing?" Jake asked. Bobby ignored him. The apostle was huddled over this stone, chanting some gibberish.

"Ozimadus, guide us on our mission," Bobby whispered. "We are at your mercy." He went on. "May we find salvation through your vision. Send us now to the Isle of Labor." The others had lay down as instructed. Jake peeped over the side and watched the reef below begin to glow, filling the sea with light. The glow spread through the reef in both directions as far as Jake could see, perhaps circling the island. The boat began to shake. Jake lay down. There was a brilliant flash followed by a violent jerk of the boat. Water spilled over the side. Then it became still. Everyone sat up.

"Not such a bad landing," said Bobby.

"What happened?" Jake asked. He looked over and could make out the outline of a tall, dark wall in the distance with a bronze glow above it.

"We've arrived at the Isle of Labor," said Bobby. "The largest island in Limbo!"

"How are we going to get over those walls?" Jake asked.

"We don't have to go over them," said Bobby. "There should be an entrance near here. Let's start rowin' in that direction." Bobby pointed up the island.

They rowed past the dark, foreboding walls which appeared to be over a hundred feet high. The wall hugged the shoreline and there was only a thin, rocky outcrop below. After what seemed an eternity of rowing they came upon a large archway lit by a flaming cauldron on each side. The water ran under the arch and through to the other side of the wall.

"Row to the entrance," said Bobby. "Keep the canoes together. When I give ya the word everybody lay down and cover yourselves."

The group paddled hard for the great arch. The flames of the cauldron brilliantly lit the waters churning through the entrance, giving them a brilliant, red shine.

"Now!" Bobby cried. Everyone ducked as Bobby guided the two canoes through the channel, straining to hold the boats together. A small rock jutting out of the water ahead held a sentinel, stepping from a small guardhouse.

"Bobby of Birmingham. 277423," Bobby yelled back. The canoes were almost even with the sentinel's lonely post. The sentinel, in his long black cloak, entered the guardhouse and seconds later walked back out.

"Pass on brother. May ye rest from your journey."

"Bless thee brother, bless thee," Bobby responded. The canoes slid onward into the bay.

Jake peeped out. He saw several buildings and smokestacks surrounded by an orange glow beyond the bay. He quickly ducked back down. Bobby paddled the canoes to the shore. Several other canoes and sailboats were beached there. There was no sign of anyone around.

"Okay now, boys, and ladies. Help me get ashore here," Bobby said, jumping into the knee-deep water. The rest of the group silently slid into the water and began pulling the boats onto the rocky shoreline.

"Stay down. I'll be right back," Bobby whispered. He walked quickly toward a small, black building a few yards away.

Jake looked around and carefully took in his surroundings. Around the entire bay was the outline of something that looked like the industrial age gone mad. Row upon row of cloud-spewing smokestacks, great turning iron wheels and rusted metal machinery was stacked to the horizon. Sounds of machines filled the air. A short wall circled the bay and the small building on the shore.

"Be quick now everyone!" Bobby whispered from one end of the building. "Get in here!"

Jake and David scampered up the shore, followed by Singing Wind and Red Moon. Bobby was holding a door open.

"Come! Come! Come!" the apostle hurried them in.

Inside, the cramped room was barren except for a few crates at the end of an open, wooden floor surrounded by dark, windowless walls. Bobby closed the door behind them and ran over to one of the crates, lifting its cover. He pulled a dark, cloth object out.

"Come now! Everyone gits one!" He handed the black robe to Red Moon, who quickly slipped into the apostle garb. "We gotta fit in if we're gonna move around here!"

They were quickly dressed and ready.

"Let's go. Back outside now," said Bobby.

"Where?" said Jake.

"To find Mister Menon, of course!" the leering apostle said.

"Why don't we stay here until daybreak." David said.

"Nope! Too dangerous! Other brothers will be comin' and goin'. We must go out into the factories."

Bobby led the way to the door. Everyone pulled the hoods over their heads and followed him out. Bobby let the group to a large, stone door in the wall around the bay. There was a combination lock embedded in the stone. Bobby leaned in close to the lock.

"Just a darn minute and I'll have us in." He twirled the dial, straining to see the numbers. He stood back and pushed the door. It held fast.

"Damn this thing. I can never remember it!" he complained.

"You hurry, Bobby. More boats coming," Singing Wind said, looking back at the bay.

Coming through the giant arch of the great wall, they could see several canoes and a couple of small said boats sliding into the bay. They were full of apostles.

"I wonder if they're good brothers or bad," Bobby said.

"I don't want to find out!" Jake cried. "Get this damn door open, now!"

Bobby wiped his brow and leaned back down, thumbing the dial.

"Boats getting closer," said Singing Wind.

"Come on Bobby!" Jake whispered urgently. The lock clicked and the door pushed inward. The group moved quickly inside the entrance. They were surrounded by a mass of pipes, pistons, and giant, turning wheels. Machines of all shapes and sizes hummed, groaned, and grinded away. Bobby led them down a narrow passageway between shifting cranks pulling massive pistons up and down. Jake could glimpse someone locked in solitary work every few feet. A person appeared as a dark shadow, buried in a machine and performing some lonely task. The heat was unbearable. Flames shot from pipes, giving off noxious fumes and filling the air with soot and smoke. They came to a metal, spiral staircase leading upward. Bobby grabbed the railing, signaling the others to follow.

The group began climbing the stairs. Spread beneath them was a jungle of metal and heat. Catwalks were strung all around them. Huge chains, some with hooks, were suspended from somewhere above. Another apostle was coming towards them from up above on the stairs.

"Heads down, everyone," Bobby whispered. The other apostle passed them. Bobby nodded and crossed his chest at the brother and the others did the same.

High above all the metal, Jake saw what appeared to be the tops of three mountains in the distance. A single, stone citadel stood at the top of the middle one, the glow from the factories giving it a bloody sheen.

The group left the stairwell and entered a metal catwalk which swung loosely suspended by thin rods. Other catwalks and pipes hung crazily all around. Jake looked down and spotted a large group of apostles moving in single file through the maze of machines. They were heading in the direction of the stairwell.

"How much further?" Jake asked.

"Not much," Bobby said, looking back over his shoulder.

"Where are we going?" Jake continued.

"A place to hide," said Bobby. They came to a metal wall. A catwalk ran in both directions along its sides. They turned right and came to a door. Bobby pushed it open and entered. The others followed.

Jake looked back and could see no one following. They entered a dark, damp, smelly tub of a room. Jake could feel water on the cold metal floor. Someone closed the door, plunging them into darkness. Suddenly a large, overhead light ignited. A group of apostles stood before them, several others blocking off the door behind. They were armed with large, square shields and black-bladed knives.

"Bobby, what have you done?" Jake shouted. Singing Wind and Red Moon backed into one another, bows ready. Jake and David drew their daggers. Bobby Joe turned nervously in a circle. Menon stepped out of the shadows. He was dressed in the chic attire of a 1920's Chicago gangster with his long dark hair slicked back into a ponytail. He walked up to Bobby as the apostles closed in a circle around the trapped party.

"Thank you, Bobby," said Menon. "Very good work."

"Bobby! Damn you!" Jake shouted.

Singing Wind let an arrow fly at Menon. With the speed of an atom, Menon caught the arrow in flight, stopped it inches from this thin nose. Several apostles closed in and grabbed Singing Wind. Others subdued Red Moon as she tried to help him. Jake and David were taken from behind and held firmly.

Bobby looked back at Jake.

"No, no. I didn't help them. I don't know what he's talkin' about!" Bobby shouted. "Brothers! Can't you see what this monster's done to you! Repent and cast him out!"

"Bobby! I'm shocked," Menon said. "And after all I was going to do for you." Menon stared intently into Bobby's eyes.

"You love me, don't you Bobby?" Menon asked.

"Yes," Bobby said blankly, nodding.

Menon took out a black bladed dagger.

"Show them all how much, Bobby," Menon said, handing the knife to Bobby. Bobby took the knife by its red handle and approached Jake. He held the weapon up, the overhead light glinting off it. He pointed the blade at Jake. His arm shook as he moved it toward Jake's abdomen.

"Show them all, Bobby," Menon hissed.

Bobby whirled around toward Menon.

"No, you devil!" Bobby stepped toward Menon. Bobby's arm suddenly shot up, plunging the blade into his own chest. He collapsed onto the floor. Jake and the others were horrified and struggled against their captors.

Menon walked up to Bobby whose mouth was open in shock-a last gasp of breath trying to escape.

"Obedience. That's all I ask for," said Menon.

"Damn you, devil!" Bobby said with his last living breath in Limbo.

Menon walked over and kicked Bobby's lifeless corpse as it turned to dust.

Jake and the others' hands were bound behind their backs. They were searched, their weapons removed.

"Accck!" an apostle screamed as he pulled a blue stone from Singing Wind's pouch, dropped it to the floor and clutching, his hand. A low murmur swept through the renegade apostles as they stepped back in fear.

"It's just a damn rock," Menon cried. "Bring out the gloves!" An apostle stepped forward, slipping on a pair of heavy gloves that extended to his elbows. Another apostle brought a small, wooden box forward. They deposited the blue stones into the box. Jake could tell the whole process made Menon uneasy.

"Okay, the show's over! To the tower with them!" Menon shouted.

Chapter 31

As Jake slept that night in a cell high atop the citadel, he slipped once again into the past. He found himself at the house in California. This time he stood only a few steps away from the green station wagon as it vibrated and coughed nearby, the red rag neatly stuffed into the exhaust. He looked down. He was wearing the black wetsuit, as though transported directly from the citadel. He looked over at the car. He could see his father hunched in the driver's seat. Suddenly, he saw himself, his young, frightened self entering through the side-gate, walking slowly toward the car. The boy had a look of confusion as he glanced nervously at the wagon.

Jake watched himself intently.

"Do something!" he yelled to himself, but the boy only glanced quickly at his father, a look of horror spreading over his face. The boy ran off toward the gate.

"Come back...me!" Jake screamed. The boy never heard the phantom yelling at him. Jake caught a swift glimpse of a yellow bike pedal past on the street beyond.

It's up to me, he thought. *I've got to do something now, maybe I can change everything!* He ran over to the driver's door and pulled at the door handle. It was locked. The rear door was also locked. He ran over to the front passenger side and tried. It too was locked as was the rear door. He looked around on the ground. A large rock sat nearby. He ran over and picked it up, running back and hurling it through the passenger window, shattering the glass. He reached in and unlocked the door, pulling it open. His father didn't move.

"Dad!"

There was no response. David Barr sat, eyes closed, leaning against the window glass, a stream of drool running down his chin. Jake coughed as the fumes attacked him.

He reached over and felt for his Dad's pulse. There was none.

"Dad!" he screamed again. His father didn't stir from his death sleep.

"Jake," a voice spoke from behind him. Jake spun back and saw his father standing on the grass. He was dressed in the brown worker's uniform from the Isle of Labor. Jake jumped out of the car.

"There was nothing you could have done, son. I was gone already."

"But I didn't try, I just ran away, left you there." Jake began to cry.

"It wasn't your fault, son," David said, walking up and embracing his son. The car continued to hum away. Jake looked back at the car, the window was back to normal, the door closed. Sirens screamed through the California morning air, coming closer and closer...

Jake was awakened from his slumber by David. They were still in the small, dusty cell somewhere in the citadel where they'd been marched to during the night. Singing Wind and Red Moon sat on the floor nearby, comforting each other.

"What do we do, Dad?" Jake asked.

"All we can do is wait, son. And hope."

"Hope for what?"

"A miracle," said David.

There was a small slit for a window on the far wall. Jake

walked over and peered out. The morning sun was just over the horizon, blinding him as he looked around at the huge maze of pumping machinery and smoke-spewing chimneys. Jake looked down at the base of the citadel. Small groups of people were starting to gather on the hillside. Jake saw five wooden crosses laid out at the foot of the fortress.

"There's something going on down there," Jake said.

David ran over and looked out as Jake backed up a step, a look of shock on his face. David pulled away and grabbed his son.

"Don't give up! You! Us! We've all come too far to throw in the towel," he said.

"Like you did on Earth," Jake said softly.

"No one's going to give up here, Jake! I'm with you till the end this time, buddy."

Singing Wind stood up and said, "No sweat!"

There was a sound of keys being moved and the wooden door opened. A group of apostles stood at the door brandishing black blades.

"It's time," one of the apostles said. "Don't try anything!"

The apostles first grabbed Singing Wind and then Red Moon. They were quickly bound and led out. David was taken next. He struggled and was clubbed in the back as a result. Four apostles came towards Jake.

"Turn around!" One growled. Jake turned and as the apostle moved to bind his hands, Jake swung around quickly and landed a punch to the man's face, knocking him down into the dirt floor. The other three apostles dived onto Jake and pinned him as he wrestled fruitlessly to fight back. He was bound and marched outside, through a hallway and down a flight of stone steps.

Jake was led into a large, windowless room lit by flaming

torches. The rest of his group stood next to a great wooden door. They were being guarded by a large group of apostles circling the room. Menon strode in, pulling a woman along behind him. He held a chain tied to a ring around her neck. The woman had dirty, blonde hair and wore a short white skirt. She looked miserable, her feet bare and cut.

"Say hello to our guests, Norma Jean," Menon said, pulling the woman forward. The woman only managed a slight smile and a nod. "Marilyn's being a little shy," Menon said.

Menon strode up to Jake and his group. "You've all been found guilty of treason, espionage, sedition, and just bad manners, to put it lightly. How do you plead?"

"I want a lawyer," said Jake. The apostles in the room laughed, angering Menon.

"I'll do the jokes here, thank you!" Menon growled. "I'll give you all one last chance to join me. The alternative outside is not going to be pretty!"

No one spoke or stirred.

"Very well! Bring out the other prisoner to join her friends!" Menon snapped. A door flew open and Emily was led out kicking and screaming. She stopped when she saw Jake.

"Jake!" She broke free and ran to him, embracing him tightly.

"Didn't think I'd forget and leave you here, did you?" Jake said.

"Oh, Jake," she said, as they were pulled apart.

"Oh, Jake!" Menon mocked in a feminine voice. "You two make me wanna puke! Outside with them all! It's curtain time!"

They were each marched outside and placed in front of a wooden cross which lay on the ground behind them.

Holes had been dug for the crosses to be positioned in. Jake was put in the middle with Singing Wind and Red Moon to his right, Emily and David to the left. The crowd below had grown considerably. It was a dirty, rag-tag mob. Their clothes were covered in grime and sweat. Looks of despair were fixed on their faces. A long line of apostles formed a chain in front of the crowd. Jake was untied and placed upon the cross by two apostles who held an arm. A third apostle grabbed his feet, pulled them down. Jake looked back. A man with a large mallet stood next to a large pile of stakes. He wore a black cloak, and a dark hood covered his head. Jake watched as Menon strode to the front of the crowd.

"Ladies, and gentlemen! We are gathered here to witness the execution of these five traitors who would take away all the reforms that I have made possible for you!" A low murmur went through the crowd. Menon continued, "They would take away the reforms I have started!" The crowd grew uneasy, some shouting, "Kill them!" as others threw fruit at the captives.

"Reforms such as breaks!" Light applause came from the crowd. "I have allowed you to have sex here!" More scattered applause echoed through the crowd. "No more feeling guilty about how you got to this place!" Menon put his hands together and egged on the crowd, waving.

Jake pulled free from the three apostles and stood up. "He's lying!" Jake shouted. "He means to keep you here forever! At least before, you had a chance to leave here when your time is up!"

"Someone shut him up!" Menon bellowed. The crowd was buzzing at Jake's words. "Some deliverer! At least the one on Earth could walk on water!" Menon played to the crowd.

"Him walk on water too!" Singing Wind spoke up.

"Huh?" Menon looked surprised for a moment. "Shut that one up too!"

The three apostles recaptured Jake and forced him back down onto the cross as he struggled.

"Don't listen to him!" Jake cried from his prone position. An apostle ran up and gagged Jake's mouth with a dirty, red rag. It smelled of smoke.

"Executioner, do your duty," Menon said casually.

The hooded man reached down and pulled up a handful of stakes. He walked up to where Jake was lying. A warm breeze ran over the hill and Jake heard the sound of metal tinkling nearby. The executioner's robe opened slightly and Jake saw the dog-tags glimmer in the sunlight.

"Now!" Newt shouted, throwing the hood off his head.

"What?!!" cried Menon. "Someone stop them!"

Suddenly hundreds of workers poured over the hill from the other side, carrying makeshift weapons of all types. Others ran out of the crowd and began to subdue the wayward apostles. Newt whipped the mallet into the face of one the apostles holding down Jake, sending the man flying. Jake stood up and punched another. Workers converged on the hill, freeing the others. Apostles fought against apostles.

Most of the workers on the hillside retreated back down into the factories. The renegade apostles were captured, while the remaining retreated into the citadel, barring the door from inside.

"Where's Menon?" Jake yelled as his father came up to him.

"He must be inside," David said. Newt approached with a big smile on his face.

"Newt! How did you?" Jake asked, hugging his friend.

"With a little help from a gook!" Newt answered. "Tom! Thomas!" Newt yelled. An apostle, hood down, ran up to them. "This is Thomas of Milwaukee! He got me here!"

"Glad to meet ya," Thomas said. He was a heavy-set man with playful, dark eyes.

A group of workers had grabbed one of the wooden crosses and began to ram the doors of the citadel. Jake found Emily in all the chaos.

"Are you okay?" Jake asked.

"Yes. I'm okay," she said.

"Did he hurt you?"

"No. He said you were dead and gone back to Earth. He kept telling me you'd failed."

The door of the citadel crashed inward, and with a roar the workers and good apostles rushed inside led by Newt and Thomas. A heavy, vibrating noise suddenly filled the air around the citadel. Jake looked up to see a black helicopter lift off the citadel's roof, speeding off for the horizon.

"Where in the hell did he get a helicopter from?" Jake asked.

"That was the first one," a nearby worker said. "He had us building a fleet of them."

Minutes later Newt came running out, followed by Thomas.

"Menon's gone!" Newt cried.

"I think I know where he's going," said Thomas.

"Where?" asked Jake.

"The Angel's Isle."

Chapter 32

"But we can only travel at night," Jake said.

"On the contrary, my strangely dressed friend," Thomas said. "That's only for traveling from anywhere but here. We can leave from the Isle of Labor at any time."

"How?" Jake asked.

"You will see, soon enough," said Thomas.

The situation on the hill had stabilized. The majority of the crowd dispersed. The renegade apostles had been subdued and their black blades confiscated. Newt excused himself, saying he had to go for some of his "things." Singing Wind and Red Moon began to craft bows from the wooden crosses. David talked quietly with a friend he had worked with on the Isle. Emily stayed close to Jake's side.

"You aren't leaving now, are you Jake?" Emily asked.

"I'm not going to leave you again if I can help it. I promise you," said Jake.

Newt ran up, a large object in his arms. It was the glowboard.

"I thought you might want this," Newt said.

Jake was delighted. "Didn't think I'd see this again," he said, taking the board from Newt.

Even in the bright sunlight, Jake could tell the board was humming with a soft glow as though it had found its owner.

"Thomas told me you're leaving this place," said Newt. "Going back to Earth. I thought you might have time for another night surf before you leave."

"Thanks Newt. But tell me, how did you get here? How

did you get together with Thomas? And how did you get away from those demons back at your house?"

"Never underestimate a United States Marine," Newt said, beaming. "I held those creatures off as long as I could. I killed a bunch of 'em, but then I lost my weapon. That's when they chased me outside. Last thing I remember was them surrounding me and then I woke up in my bed."

"So the resurrection stories are true then," said Jake.

"You doubted me?" said Emily.

"I've doubted everything in this place," said Jake. "Then what happened, Newt?"

"I made a raft. Never trusted that guy at the dock. Figured him for a gook informer. Anyway, I put in the water and started rowing in the direction I saw the balloon headin', when a long comes one of these bald guys in a canoe. That's when I met Thomas. He converted me."

"Converted? You mean in the religious sense?"

"Yep. I'm a new man," said Newt, scratching himself. "It's just devil's we're fightin', no gooks. I hear they can make me an M-16 here! Rather have Charlie's AK-47 though. Hell of a gun!"

"I don't think we need an arms race here," said Jake.

"Right you are there, Jake," laughed Thomas. "We'll soon have all the workers back producing what they were before."

"Which is?" said Jake.

"Nothing," replied Thomas.

Jake noticed the woman Menon had called Norma Jean moving off down the hillside. *Could that really be the same Marilyn from Earth? At least she's free from Menon.*

"I actually got here before you did," said Newt.

"What did you do when you got here?" asked Jake.

"Well, me and Thomas, we hid in the mines. They're

at the base of the two other mountains. The workers are real ornery down there. They revolt every other day. It was no problem raisin' us a little army. Our spies watched 'em march you guys into the fort here."

"You did good, Newt," said Jake.

Two apostles walked up. They were carrying the weapons that had been previously taken away the night before. Another apostle followed with a box.

"Our stuff," said Jake. He yelled to Singing Wind and Red Moon to stop their cutting and claim their bows.

"Your lights, too," said Thomas. "We have plenty here we could have given you. It looks like we're ready to leave now."

"To see the Angel of Limbo," said Jake.

Thomas led Jake's group down through the factories. Shortly, they came to a small, round, white-brick building. A long row of canoes stood outside.

"Two should be enough," Thomas said, inspecting the canoes. Thomas grabbed the rear of one canoe. David and Singing Wind went to a second. Newt took the front of Thomas's canoe, leaving Jake with Emily and Red Moon.

"Be a sport and get the door, will you Jake?" said Thomas. Jake walked over to the white, wooden, double doors and opened them. It was pitch dark inside.

"We're going in here?" asked Jake.

"That's right," said Thomas. "I don't know how fast that machine Menon was in can go, but if we hurry inside we may just beat him. Here Jake, catch!" Thomas tossed a blue stone at Jake. "Lead the way, please."

Jake hesitated for a second. As the stone began to glow, he stepped inside. There was a slight decline that turned into water. It was like an indoor swimming pool. Jake stepped aside as the two canoes passed through.

The group boarded the canoes. Jake and Emily shared a canoe with Singing Wind and Red Moon, the three other men climbed into the other canoe. Jake laid the glowboard against one side of the canoe.

"But...?" Jake began to ask.

"I know it may seem a little strange, but if you look down you will see the bottom is coated with the same blue rock as the reed and stone in your hand," said Thomas.

Jake looked around at the white walls which rose up to a white curved dome ceiling, the light and ripples reflecting there on the painting of a woman. She was flying through the heavens, half naked with long shrouds of white cloth wrapped around her body.

"Everyone please lay back in the canoes," Thomas said. "Is everyone ready? Well then, if no one's backing out then it's off we go. I love this part." Thomas bowed his head and muttered from gibberish, followed by, "Ozimadus, guide us to your home. We are at your mercy. May we find salvation through your vision," followed by more gibberish. The entire room began to glow with a blinding, blue light. Jake looked up as the woman above smiled brilliantly down upon him. *Could that be the Angel? Had some mad artist seen her face?*

The boats seemed to be spinning slowly, the whole pool became a mild whirlpool as the lady above flew on her journey. Suddenly the boats lurched sharply. Blinding sunlight rained down upon the two boats.

"We have arrived," said Thomas.

Chapter 33

The sound of birds filled the air. Jake and the others rose and looked about. They were sitting in a calm sea, the canoes gently rocking alongside one another. Before them was a green coastline with brilliant flowers of all colors hanging in the trees. There were no beach homes to be seen.

"The river empties out just ahead. Let's row," said Thomas.

"Where does the river lead to?" asked Jake.

"To the Angel's palace," answered Thomas.

They began rowing up the coast. Birds of all types flew above, circling the trees on the shoreline. In the grass under the trees, Jake spotted a couple of horses quietly grazing. Singing Wind spotted a deer nearby.

"Why are there animals here?" Jake asked.

"'Why' is a good question," said Thomas. "Perhaps this island is a small slice of Heaven. The animals here don't fear man. It's like the Garden of Eden all over again." Singing Wind lowered his bow which he had been aiming at the deer.

"It's beautiful," said Emily.

The boats came upon a wide, river-mouth. They steered the canoes into the mouth and rowed upstream against a weak current. On both sides of the river a wide grassy plain extended several hundred yards until it reached the woods. Animals of all types grazed peacefully or played on both sides of the river. Red Moon pointed anxiously at a small group of elephants dousing themselves in the shallow near the shore. Emily screamed as a hippo emerged by her canoe and opened its mouth, exposing a wide cave of teeth. It quickly sank and disappeared.

"What was that?" Emily said, shaking.

"Just a hippo," said David, laughing at her.

"This is like the hunting ground in the sky my grandfather always told me about," said Singing Wind. Red Moon nodded in agreement.

"Except you can't hunt here," said Thomas. "Eating fruit will have to do. This place is like one, big, petting zoo." An eagle swooped low and checked out the travelers. Two lions wrestled playfully on the nearby bank.

Suddenly all the creatures on both sides of the bank stiffened and looked toward the sky. Everyone stopped rowing and listened. The faint but growing sound of helicopter rotors could be heard. The animals began to stampede, most running away up the bank. Others headed off sideways toward the woods while some leaped headlong into the river.

Singing Wind was the first to spot the chopper coming in low on the horizon and following the river upstream. The black humming object drove all life before it. Singing Wind readied an arrow as the copter came in over the canoes. The arrow flew, bouncing harmlessly off the bottom as the chopper slowed and hovered above. The wind from the blades rocked the canoes back and forth, the noise of the rotors deafening everyone's shouts. Red Moon stood up and dived into the water. Singing Wind followed. Menon stuck his head out the side and laughed hideously. The black chopper turned and sped off upriver.

The heads of the two Indians popped up as the chopper disappeared. Jake pulled Red Moon aboard. Singing Wind pulled himself in behind as Emily helped.

"What type of bird was that?" queried the drenched Singing Wind. Red Moon shivered behind him.

"A bird we're gonna kill!" shouted Newt.

"Those were things built by men after your time on Earth," said Jake. "To let men fly in the sky."

"Why man want to fly?" asked Singing Wind. "He just get in bird's way." They began to row upstream again.

"You said you knew Menon would be coming here, Thomas," Jake said. "It looks like you were right."

"Yes, I was," Thomas answered.

"How did you know? I don't want to be lead into a trap again," said Jake.

"I was here when Menon first appeared," answered Thomas. "The vortex is here."

"Vortex?"

"The gateway to Hell. Limbo and Hell became linked here. I was working the palace grounds, keeping the rhinos away from the hedges."

"Hedges?" said Jake.

"It's a hedge maze, like that of an English castle. That's where the vortex appeared. Menon came walking out followed by some winged demon. The vortex must be inside the maze. I think he's going back there to re-group."

"Then we're too late," said Jake.

"Let's hope not," answered Thomas.

Above the trees, around a bend in the river, Jake could see the top of the palace. The others saw it too. There was a single, blue shard glittering in the sky. As they rounded the bend they came upon a large blue lake, the blue crystal palace shining upon its bank.

"The holy lake," said Singing Wind.

"From the book I read him," laughed Newt.

They rowed across the lake. The palace looking down

upon them appeared like several, large shards of blue crystals stuck into the ground without any real symmetry. They came ashore on a grass lawn and left the boats. The black helicopter sat empty nearby. Jake grabbed the glowboard and helped Emily ashore.

"The maze is in the back," Thomas said.

"I want to look inside first," said Jake. "I'll catch up. Emily can come with me."

"Very well," said Thomas. "The rest of you come with me."

"Be careful, son," David said.

"I will. You be careful, Dad."

Thomas led the others around the palace and out of sight, leaving Jake and Emily alone. Two, large, bronze doors beckoned in front of them. Jake led Emily to the entrance.

"Will it be safe, Jake?"

"You're with Jake Barr, remember?"

Jake pulled one of the massive doors open, feeling a sweet-smelling breeze spill out. It was the smell of perfume.

They stepped into a massive hall covered with green, marble stone. Massive columns rose up out of sight, shrouded in mists. Jake heard a voice somewhere. They walked behind one of the pillars and kept close to the wall. Again they could hear a voice. Jake peered around the column and saw a figure dressed in black standing next to a tall, glass object shaped like an oversized mason jar. A man sat inside the jar. The other glass cells sat nearby, also containing one man each.

"You now!" the figure in black commanded. "It is your turn." It was the voice of a woman, dressed in a floor-length black dress, a dark veil covering her face.

"Neptune's Waltz," the man in the jar near her replied. It was Percy's voice!

"A man came dancing across the sea,
I'm looking for answers he said to me,
He'd risen from a kingdom of fish and shells,
wanting to learn of Heaven and Hell.
I said in the light he'd see many things,
mostly man's creations and misery.
"Go back to your paradise deep," I said to him…
"No one has the answers who walks on the ground."
He turned and danced back, sinking…with not a sound."

Shelley's voice faded away. The lady in black twirled in a circle. "Wonderful!" she shouted. "Someone else now!" She danced around and turned another circle.

"Shelley's a prisoner. I've got to free him," Jake whispered to Emily. Jake felt a hand on his back. He turned and found Red Moon behind him.

"You hurry, Jake! They need you!" she said urgently. Red Moon turned back toward the entrance.

"But Shelley…," Jake said after her. He grabbed Emily by the hand and followed Red Moon. Percy would have to wait.

They emerged on the lawn and began walking to the rear of the palace. The hedge-maze came into view. Red Moon led the way to an entrance in the middle of a long, green wall which stood around ten feet tall.

"The bad man run in here," Red Moon said. "They chase him." Somewhere in the maze a cry of pain rang out.

"You two stay here, I'm going in," Jake said. He was tempted to drop the glowboard, but something told him to hang on to it. He entered the maze.

Jake turned right, then left again, the maze forcing

him to choose directions. He turned left again, hitting a dead end. He heard another cry somewhere in the maze. It sounded like Newt. Jake quickly retraced his steps and ran down another path. Turning a corner, he came upon Singing Wind lying in the grass, clutching a wound.

"Two men without hair with him. Be careful Jake," Singing Wind gasped. So Menon wasn't alone.

"Hang in there buddy, I'll be back," said Jake. He ran further into the maze, frequently hitting dead ends, turning around and trying new routes. Rounding another corner he came upon Newt, sitting and holding a hand to a bloody spot on his forehead.

"Somebody whacked me good," Newt said. "I must've blacked out." Barely alive, an apostle lay nearby, a dagger sticking from his abdomen.

"You stay here and rest, pal," said Jake. "I'll get Menon for you." Jake turned and ran on. He went up and down several zig-zags, more dead ends, and then came upon Thomas lying on his back. An apostle stood over him, readying a spear for a death blow. Jake ran up and brought the glowboard down upon the man's skull. The man fell over and became still.

Jake heard his father cry out nearby.

"The vortex, it's just around the corner. Your father is in there with Menon!" Thomas gasped. Jake twirled and ran around a corner. A small glow came from a narrow break in the hedge. He stepped through the entrance.

Menon stood with his back to Jake, facing a large, round, shimmering object with no defined edges. He was softly chanting something. To his left, Jake spied his father lying in the grass, a dagger stuck in his chest.

"Dad!" Jake crouched down next to his father's side, laying the glowboard in the grass. His dad was alive. Menon heard Jake and turned. "It's okay Jake. Just stop him." Jake stood and faced Menon.

"You again!" Menon squealed. Behind Menon, Jake could see dark, ominous-looking figures poised to come walking out of the swirling vortex. They were creatures of horrible appearance and manner. Some had wings. Others had horns protruding from their heads, while still others were of shapes twisted and mangled.

Menon pulled out a long, black-bladed sword.

"Prepare to go to Hell, Jake Barr!" Menon leaped at Jake and swung, missing as Jake ducked, the blade going into the hedge. Jake swung a punch, hitting Menon in the nose, surprising him. Menon quickly brought the handle of the sword around, catching Jake on his temple.

Menon threw the sword down. Jake had collapsed into the grass.

"I don't need such simple toys to destroy you, Barr," said Menon. He raised his hands in the air a few feet apart. Suddenly a red ball of energy appeared and began spinning between his hands.

"Now you're going to feel some heat, surfer." Menon pulled one hand back and the fiery ball followed. He quickly threw his hand toward Jake. The ball spiraled at Jake who tried to block it with his outstretched hands.

"No!" David Barr shouted, throwing himself in front of his son.

The fireball smashed into David who fell back into Jake's arms.

"Dad!" Jake screamed. His father didn't respond. Jake looked up at the sneering Menon. Jake felt like a volcano about to erupt. He grabbed the glowboard, stood, and faced Menon.

"You bastard! It's over for you," Jake growled.

"Sorry, Jake, but there are no waves here," Menon laughed loudly.

Jake pointed the board at Menon and ran full speed ahead, screaming loudly. The point of the board struck Menon in the abdomen. Menon's body seemed to absorb the board. Jake let go and stepped back. Behind Menon, Jake could see the dark figures beginning to emerge.

"You insolent little brat!" Menon moaned, as the board sank deeper into his body, "I was so close, so close." Menon stepped back toward the vortex. A disfigured head emerged from the vortex behind him. Jake breathed deeply and ran once more at Menon. He pushed the board and victim into the vortex, knocking the creature back as Menon was pushed in. Menon fluttered helplessly into the void. Jake stepped back as the swirling gateway began to break up. Menon's head stuck out for an instant. He screamed horribly as a tentacle reached out and pulled him back in. The vortex burst with light and disappeared.

Jake ran over to his father. He kneeled down by David and propped him up.

"Dad?"

"It's over, Jake," his father said faintly. "I hope I'm leaving on better terms with you this time, son."

"No Dad! You're not going to die!"

"We all have to die son. Some of us more than once," David smiled and closed his eyes. Thomas and Newt stumbled in to find Jake clutching his father's clothes.

"It's okay Jake. He'll be back on the Isle of Labor where he started," Thomas said.

"You promise?"

"Hey, I'm Zen-Christian. We don't lie," replied Thomas.

"Let's go help Shelley," said Jake.

Once more, Jake and Emily entered the palace. Thomas and Newt walked ahead, Singing Wind and Red Moon bringing up the rear. They walked down through the center of the great hall, the massive columns towering above on both sides. The glass cells were just ahead now, the dancing lady in black twirled between them.

"Your holiness," Thomas said, "If I may interrupt." The lady stopped spinning and walked toward Thomas. The stench of strong perfume filled the air.

"Yes? Has the bad man gone away yet?" said Ozimadus, the Angel of Madness.

"Yes Your Holiness. Thanks to these brave souls here with me," Thomas replied gesturing at Jake and the others.

"Then they shall be rewarded," Ozimadus said.

"Release Shelley!" Jake blurted out.

"Jake. Please," Thomas said.

The men in the glass cells rose to their feet. Shelley waved at Jake and Emily.

"Disband my collection of poets?" the Angel asked.

"Yes," Jake answered.

"Very well. They are beginning to bore me anyway. I think I'll collect soldiers now," she smiled. Newt shuffled his feet. Ozimadus twirled quickly and the glass around the poets vanished. Shelley and the others walked quickly over to the group.

"Thank you Jake! If I had to recite one more poem I think I would've gone mad!" Shelley cried. A dark-haired man pressed next to Percy.

"This is my friend George Byron," said Shelley. "Jake Barr, this is the one," Shelley said to Byron, who nodded his approval. "And Keats, Longfellow, Yeats, and Whitman there."

"Thank you," the bards all said in unison.

"Jake Barr, it is time for you to leave," the Angel said, spinning into the crowd. "Your friends will all be rewarded for their heroism." She looked at Newt and Singing Wind. "I'll need a couple of hunters to catch some flying pets the bad man left here. How about you two?"

"Yes," said Newt. Singing Wind nodded in agreement.

"Thomas, you will now be my head apostle."

"Thank you, Your Holiness," Thomas replied.

"Are you ready, Jake Barr? There are those who love you waiting for you back on Earth," said the Angel.

"There is someone who loves me here," Jake said. "You've forgotten her reward."

"If it is meant to be then you will meet again," said Ozimadus. "You can have a minute."

Jake and Emily embraced.

"Emily, I..."

"Don't waste words, Jake. She kissed him hard and he back as the others smiled approvingly. The Angel began to twirl around them as their long kiss ended.

"It is time. It is time," the Angel repeated in her dance.

Emily looked down and pulled something out of her pocket.

"Hold on to this," she said, putting the object into Jake's hand.

"What is it?" Jake looked down at the small heart-shaped, metal object.

"Just hold it tightly, my love! So you'll never forget!" Emily cried.

Jake was beginning to fade. Byron leaped forward. "Revive Romanticism! Revive Romanticism, Jake Barr!" Byron shouted. Shelley pulled him back. Jake shook his head in confusion.

His friends waved and said good-bye. Jake felt tears run down his cheeks. "Good-bye!" he said. *Is this dream really ending?* He looked at Emily.

"I love you," her fading image spoke. "I love you too," he said. All went dark.

Epilogue

Howard Robinson was making his 6 AM, bed-check. It had been a long night. Mr. Thompson had the runs and Mrs. Langley kept getting out of her bed and walking the halls. And then there was the storyteller, Jake Barr.

Howard stopped at room 40 and cracked Jake's door open. The bed was empty. "Damn Jake, gotta put you back in bed too!" Howard entered the room. Jake was gone. Howard looked quickly over to the corner of the room. The surfboard was gone!

Howard ran out of the room and down the hallway, into the head nurse's office.

"Call the police! Jake Barr's gone!" Howard shouted at the plump, little lady eating doughnuts.

"Where's he gone?" she said, almost choking.

"He's gone surfin'!" Howard cried.

"Surfing?" The nurse raised an eyebrow.

"Just tell the cops to go to the beach down the street! I'm sure he's there!" Howard ran out.

A small crowd had gathered at the shore. Howard ran out on the beach, his black loafers lifting great whiffs of sand in his wake. The people on the beach were pointing and laughing.

"Look at the old man," a small boy said.

Howard followed the kid's finger out to the sea. There was old Jake, bony legs straddling his board, waiting for the next set to come in.

"He's gonna die!" a skinny teen laughed. "There are big waves coming in."

Howard ran back and forth trying to catch Jake's attention. "Jake! Jake come in!"

Jake noticed Howard, smiled hugely and waved.

A police saucer zoomed in over the crowd. Two cops in the craft's bubble could be seen. The saucer moved out over the water.

"You there!" a speaker from the saucer sounded. The police were now directly over Jake. "Head for the shore!" the cops yelled again. Jake paddled away, further out to sea.

Howard could see a large wave forming on the horizon. "No Jake. Don't do it. Paddle in!"

The saucer followed Jake. "Head for the shore!" the cops ordered. Jake paddled for the incoming wave. The large blue hill was almost upon him. The people on the beach began to shout and bounce up and down. The wave broke and Jake disappeared. Suddenly he reappeared, standing and surfing down the wave's face. The wave curled over and slammed into him as he tried to outrun the lip. He vanished into a great explosion of white foam and spray.

"Oh shit!" Howard cried.

The cops helped Howard pull Jake out of the water as the crowd gathered around. They laid Jake on his back and began CPR. Howard stood by nervously and watched. Jake opened his eyes.

"Jake?" Howard leaned over.

"It was great Howard..." Jake gurgled up some water. "I told you this was my year." Jake gurgled up some blood.

"Do something for him!" Howard yelled.

"The sky AMB is on the way," one cop said.
"Howard?"
"Yes Jake, I'm here."
"Revive Romanticism," Jake Barr said with his last dying breath.
"What?" Howard said. "Jake! Mr. Barr!" The sky AMB came into view and hovered over them.

They'd given Howard a box and told him to go clean out room 40. A new patient would be arriving the next day.

He set the trophy inside. A few of Jake's clothes were in a box under the bed. Howard pulled the box out and sat it next to the trophy box. There was another small box under the bed. Howard pulled the red, wooden box out and opened the latched covering. He reached in and picked up a small, heart-shaped locket. There was a grainy, black and white photo of a girl standing next to a tree. She had long brown hair and wore a dress down to her ankles. *Who's that? Maybe, his mom?* He reached down and pulled out a small notebook.

"The Diary of Jake Barr. My Adventures in Limbo," Howard read. He opened the notebook. Amongst a lot of scribbling were some decent drawings of an Indian, a man wearing camouflage, and a very old-looking man. Howard closed the notebook. *Could it have really all happened?* There was one more object in the red box. It was round and sat inside a cloth covering.

Howard picked up the black cloth bag, reached inside and pulled out a small, blue stone. It felt warm and reassuring. *He kept talkin' about some weird rocks. Ahh, it's just a rock.* Howard began to put the stone back into its cloth cover. He had it halfway in when it began to glow.

"Huhhh!" he said, surprised. He pulled the stone back out and held it in front of his eyes. He looked deep into the glowing, blue sphere and swore he could see the sea inside. A tiny man surfed along a wave as a woman stood waving from a white, sandy beach nearby. Howard pressed his eye closer. Tears fell down on the diary. The image began to fade as the stone slowly dimmed in his hands.

PHILLIP COTHRAN is a former resident of the Hawaiian Isles. He currently lives in Middle Tennessee where he is still searching for a good surf spot.

Coming soon...
The sequel to "Surfing Heaven"...
"Limbo's Child"
Jake and Emily's child-the first ever birth in Limbo, sets off a power struggle and new adventures, including a visit to the Isle of Children...

Made in the USA
Columbia, SC
06 July 2024